The Soy DECEPTION

David Brownstein, M.D. & Sheryl Shenefelt, C.N.

For further copies of **The Soy Deception:**

Order online: www.drbrownstein.com or www.aplacetobe.com

Call: **1-888-647-5616** or send a check or money order in the amount of: $20.00 ($15.00 plus $5.00 shipping and handling), or for Michigan residents $20.90 ($15.00 plus $5.00 shipping and handling, plus $.90 sales tax) to:

>Healthy Living
>964 Floyd Street
>Birmingham, Michigan 48009

The Soy Deception

Copyright © 2011
by David Brownstein, M.D. and Sheryl Shenefelt, C.N.
All Rights Reserved
No part of this book may be reproduced without written consent from the publisher.

ISBN: 978-0-9840869-1-7

Medical Alternatives Press
(248) 851-3372
(888) 647-5616

Center for Holistic Medicine
(248) 851-1600

A Place to Be, LLC
(248) 766-2425

Acknowledgements

David Brownstein, M.D.

I gratefully acknowledge the help I have received from my friends and colleagues in putting this book together. This book could not have been published without help from the editors—my wife, Allison, and my chief editor, Janet Darnell. Sheryl, it is always a pleasure to work with you. I have learned much from you.

Of course, to my patients—THANK YOU! Without your support and search for safe and effective natural treatments, none of this would be possible. I believe in you and I thank you for believing in me.

Sheryl Shenefelt, C.N.

I want to express my deep gratitude to my husband Bob and to my family for their unwavering support as I pursue my passion of health and wellness. I am honored to write this book with Dr. Brownstein and work with him and his partners at The Center for Holistic Medicine. Thank you, also, to Dr. Brownstein's wife Allison and to Janet Darnell for their help with all of our books. Finally, to my patients, newsletter readers, and class attendees I appreciate you believing in me and for all of your support!

How to Utilize this Book

The following questions will be answered:

- ➢ Is soy a health food?

- ➢ What items contain soy?

- ➢ Is fermented soy good for you?

Supporters claim soy can provide an ideal source of protein, lower cholesterol, protect against cancer and heart disease, reduce menopausal symptoms, and prevent osteoporosis - among many other things. It seems like a miracle, right? Or, are there problems with soy? We will show you that soy is not a miraculous food and, furthermore, show you the other side of soy—the side the soy industry does not want you to know about. This book will expose the soy deception and give you the truth about soy.

In this book you will find research and frequently asked questions about soy, along with recipes, to help you make the best choices. Soy is in many packaged foods, flours, dressings, and sauces, as well as hidden in items we would not think to check, such as vitamins or shampoo. As a health conscious consumer, it is important to be fully informed. Use this book to help you start asking the right questions about the soy industry and its proclamations about soy. This will enable you to make an educated decision on whether to include soy in your diet.

It is always important to ask questions at restaurants and read food labels to see if soy is one of the ingredients. Many products that you think to be soy-free are not. Many companies change ingredients in their products throughout the year, so it is important to read labels often. Use this book to find out where soy is found, what names it is hidden under, and what forms of soy (if any) to include in your diet.

More about soy and this book at www.thesoydeception.com

A Word of Caution to the Reader

The information presented in this book is based on the training and professional experience of the authors. The advice in this book should not be undertaken without first consulting a physician. Proper laboratory and clinical monitoring is essential to achieving the goal of finding safe and effective natural treatments. This book was written for informational and educational purposes only. It is not intended to be used as medical advice.

Dedications

David Brownstein, M.D.

To the women of my life: Allison, Hailey, and Jessica, with all my love.

Sheryl Shenefelt, C.N.

All my love to my wonderful husband Bob and to my beautiful children Grace and Nicholas for all of their support and patience.

Thank you to Angela Biggs for your hard work on our book covers, editing, and for always being there for us.

And, to our dear friend, Dr. Robert Radtke, who taught us to ask questions and keep searching for solutions. You will be missed, Rob.

Contents

Preface		11
Chapter 1:	About Soy	15
Chapter 2:	Fermented Versus Non-Fermented Soy	31
Chapter 3:	Why Avoid Soy?	47
Chapter 4:	Soy and Phytoestrogens	61
Chapter 5:	Soy and the Thyroid	73
Chapter 6:	Soy Formula	87
Chapter 7:	Soy and Allergies	101
Chapter 8:	Soy and Genetically Modified Foods	113
Chapter 9:	Tips and Recipes	125
	Appendix A: Soy Descriptions	161
	Appendix B: Soy-Free Start-Up Shopping Guide	171
	Appendix C: Soy-Free Restaurant Guide	175
	About the Authors	179

Preface
David Brownstein, M.D.

I am continually amazed by the misinformation about soy propagated by the media. The media wants us to believe that eating more and more soy will make us healthier. I can assure you that is not true.

There are multiple varieties of soy including milk, hot dogs, spreads, butter, and oil readily available at nearly every grocery store across the United States. My experience has clearly shown that, compared to patients who do not ingest soy, those patients that ingest the most soy have more thyroid problems and more severe imbalances in their hormonal systems. In fact, I have found it nearly impossible to balance the thyroid and the rest of the endocrine system in those patients who ingest large amounts of soy in their diet.

After taking dietary histories from patients for nearly 20 years, I can assure the reader that you are what you eat. I write my books, blog, newsletters, and articles as well as lecture to help patients and professionals find what promotes health and what to avoid. I cannot emphasize enough how important it is to eat a healthy diet. As you will see in this book, eating a healthy diet means avoiding all sources of non-fermented soy.

It is up to you, the reader, to make the final choices regarding your health care decisions. You are responsible for maintaining your health. Furthermore, you are what you eat. Reading this book will give you the knowledge that you need to optimize your health.

Don't believe the media, believe in yourself.

To All Of Our Health,

[signature: David Brownstein]

David Brownstein, M.D

www.drbrownstein.com

Preface
Sheryl Shenefelt, C.N.

I always remind my patients how important it is to be an educated consumer. The media and the soy proponents would have us believe that soy is a magic bean and a miracle food. Not only that, but others say it will protect us from cancer and can save the world from hunger. This is what the media and soy propaganda has lead many consumers to believe about soy. Hence, many people have stopped eating meat and dairy and are now consuming soy milk, tofurky, and soy burgers on a daily basis. Soy is also a very cheap crop to grow and it has found its way into countless food items and dairy products, not to mention cosmetics, shampoos, and vitamins. Therefore, many people are exposed to soy on a daily basis without knowing it! However, what if people found out soy wasn't such a "miracle food" after all?

As I learned more about the "dark side" of soy through such publications as Kaayla Daniel's wonderful book **The Whole Soy Story,** as well as the alerts put out by the Weston A. Price Foundation (www.westonaprice.org), I knew we needed to write a book for our patients informing them about soy. We continue to see people who are quite sick and have hormonal and thyroid issues who are consuming excessive amounts of soy thinking it is a health food. The only soy (if any) we recommend are the fermented forms of soy discussed in this book (e.g., miso, natto, tempeh). Furthermore, we only recommend using small amounts of fermented soy items. We have included many recipes in this book to guide you, as well as in our other books **The Guide to Healthy Eating, 2nd Edition**, **The Guide to a Gluten-Free Diet, 2nd Edition,** and **The Guide to a Dairy-Free Diet**. This book is meant to help educate consumers, to shed some light on this "not-so-miracle" food, and to make everyone aware of the soy deception.

Be Well!

Sheryl Shenefelt, C.N.

www.aplacetobe.com

1

About Soy

Introduction

The soy industry and the media would have you believe that soy is a miracle food and that ingesting soy can help you overcome illness as well as enable you to obtain your optimal health. However, the most widely available forms of soy (non-fermented soy) are not healthy for you!

Soy is the cheapest crop to grow in the U.S. In 2009, the U.S. produced about 3,359 million bushels of soy, mostly in the Midwest. According to the USDA's Economic Research Service, the farm value of U.S. soybean production in 2008-09 was $29.6 billion; the second-highest value among U.S. produced crops, trailing only corn. Billions of dollars have gone into researching, manufacturing, and advertising soy-based products and world soybean production has increased by over 500 percent in the last 40 years.

The soy industry clearly has a vested interest in promoting wider uses of soy. However, there is an underside to the soy story that shines a different light on soy. The soy industry does not want the negative effects of soy exposed. This book will show you how we have been deceived by the media and the soy industry.

Information about soy is presented in this book to help you make an informed decision about whether soy, in any form, should be included in your diet.

In recent years, soy has become popular in North America as a so-called "healthy" food and has become a mainstay for vegetarians and vegans as a meat and dairy alternative. Actually, it became a staple in hospital and school lunch programs as early as the 1920s. Soy has been used in the Orient for centuries. The Orient primarily uses soy in its fermented form. In the U.S. the most common form of soy it the non-fermented form. It is important to point out that, contrary to popular belief, soy is not (and was not) consumed in large amounts in traditional Asian cultures; rather it is primarily used as a condiment.

To be clear, there are two groups of soy we will be discussing in this book: fermented and non-fermented soy. Fermentation alters the characteristics of the soybean by producing positive changes using actions produced with certain bacteria, molds, and yeasts, thus making it healthier by neutralizing soy's many inherent toxins. Non-fermented soy has not been put through this process and has many potential adverse effects as discussed in Chapter 3. In this book, when we refer to soy, we are referring to non-fermented soy. Soy that has been fermented will be referred to as fermented soy. More information on these two types of soy can be found in Chapter 2. This first chapter will give you an overview of soy, as well as information about where soy is found in food and non-food items.

Frequently Asked Questions

Why Is Soy Considered Such A Health Food Today?

Soybeans can grow under many environmental conditions and they are a fast-growing bean which can result in large yields. All these factors allow soy to be a profitable plant. From a financial standpoint, soy is an ideal crop. The soy industry is very powerful and they successfully lobbied the FDA to endorse the ingestion of soy as a way to reduce the risk of heart disease. This led to an industry explosion for soy-based products. Consider the health claim the FDA approved for soy foods in 1999:

> "Diets low in saturated fat and cholesterol that include 25 grams of soy protein a day may reduce the risk of heart disease."

The soy industry continually puts out research proclaiming a variety of health benefits linked to soy. Soy has been promoted as being able to do everything from lowering cholesterol and saturated fats in the diet, to helping save the world from hunger. The media is fed this information from the industry which reaches the public. This book will shed a different light on soy and provide you the truth behind the soy deception.

What Is The History Of Soy?

Many believe soy has been around since the beginning of time. It is speculated that the soy plant was originally used as a nitrogen-fixing agent to help other crops grow. Soy was not used as a food until fermentation was discovered by the Chinese sometime during the Chou Dynasty (1134-246 B.C.). During this period, the Chinese discovered the use of the fermentation process to make soybean paste. Fermentation refers to the growth of microorganisms in food. Common fermented Western foods and beverages are beer, wine, bread, and cheese. Natural fermentation processes help remove many of soy's naturally occurring toxins. More on fermented soy can be found in Chapter 2. The soy used in our country is primarily non-fermented soy in the form of soy protein isolate, soybean oil, and soy milk. We will show you that it is mostly the non-fermented form of soy that is causing so many health problems.

Do Asians Eat A Lot Of Soy?

The soy industry would have you believe that traditional Asian diets contained a lot of soy and that even today Asians eat large quantities of soy. Many claim that since the Asians suffer less chronic illness than most Western people, soy must be a healthy food, right? The fact is that traditional Asian diets did not and still do not contain large amounts of soy. If they do eat soy, it is usually fermented soy in small amounts. More about fermented soy can be found in Chapter 2.

How Much Soy Do Asians Actually Eat?

Traditional Asian diets included only small amounts of soy—it was used primarily as a condiment. Even today it is still not used significantly in the forms marketed to Westerners such as soy patties, tofurky, soymilk, TVP® chili, soy hot dogs, or other non-fermented forms of soy. One study found that the Chinese ate approximately two teaspoons to two tablespoons of soy/day.[1] Other research shows that Japan and China consume from 10-90 grams per day. Compare this amount of soy with a cup of tofu (250 grams) or soy milk (240 grams) both of which many Americans consume each day.

What Type Of Soy Do We Eat In The U.S?

In many Western countries, including the United States, infants may be exposed to soy formula and adults ingest soy milk or take soy isoflavone supplements. In addition, there is no shortage of other soy items—soy milk, soy cheese, soy hot dogs, soy meats, soy energy bars— as well as many other food sources. Most of these "Western" food sources contain soy protein isolate which is a highly processed, devitalized, and toxic food source that needs to be avoided. The ingesting of soy protein isolate can lead to thyroid disorders and nutrient imbalances. There is more about soy protein isolate in Chapter 2. Unfortunately, soy protein isolate is found in so many foods, we often don't even realize we are ingesting it. Furthermore, most soy, unless it is organic, is genetically modified. More on genetically modified soy can be found in Chapter 8. Finally, as compared to other crops, soy has one of the highest percentages of contamination by pesticides of any food.

What Are Common Forms of Soy Foods?

Because soy is relatively inexpensive, industry uses it in many different forms. Table 1, Page 24, lists many of the different forms of soy currently found in a variety of food items. For more detailed descriptions of various forms of soy, see Appendix A.

As previously mentioned, many vegetarians use soy in their diets. For vegetarians and vegans, some of the most popular versions of soy are tofu, soybean oil as well as spreads with soybean oil in them, meat alternatives, soy milk, and dairy alternatives. These non-fermented forms of soy contain many toxins and lead to nutrient imbalances and thyroid disorders. More on soy and the thyroid can be found in Chapter 5.

We recommend ingesting only small amounts of soy as listed in **bold** in Table 1. These are the fermented sources of soy including miso, tempeh, natto, as well as fermented soy sauce such as shoyu or tamari. The difference between fermented and non-fermented soy are discussed further in Chapter 2.

Table 1: Forms of Soy

Edamame	Soy grits
Infant formulas	Soy hulls
Hydrolyzed vegetable protein (HVP)	Soy isoflavones
	Soy isolates
Meat analogs	Soy lecithin
Miso	Soy protein concentrate
Natto	Soy protein isolate
Non-dairy soy desserts	Soy milk
Phosphatidyl serine	Soy sterols
Shoyu	Soy nuts
Soybeans (in the pod)	Soy nut butter
Soybeans (raw)	Soy sauce (non-fermented)
Soybeans (cracked/dehulled)	Soy sprouts
Soybean oil	Soy yogurt
Soy beverages	**Tamari**
Soy bran	**Tempeh**
Soy fiber – Okara, bran, isolate fiber	Textured vegetable protein (TVP®)
Soy flakes – defatted	Textured soy protein (TSP)
Soy flakes – full fat	Tofu
Soy flour	Yuba

Note: **Bolded** forms of soy are fermented

What Food Items Often Contain Soy?

Whole soybeans themselves are often eaten either boiled or roasted. Now, more than ever, soybeans are being added into a variety of items. Table 2 lists some of the food items possibly containing soy. Many top brand foods at your local grocery store contain added soy protein. However, the addition of non-fermented soy does not make the product a healthier food. In fact, it makes the food product a potentially unhealthy choice as it has many adverse effects on the body. This will be discussed further in Chapter 3. Additionally, it renders the food source a goitrogen (i.e., causes a goiter) as discussed in Chapter 5.

Soy is found in many common foods including meat and vegetarian products and, unfortunately, baby foods. According to the United Soybean Board, soybean oil accounts for 79% of the edible fats used annually in the United States. It is found in many margarines, spreads, sauces, and dressings. It is no wonder we have an epidemic of thyroid disorders.

Keep in mind non-fermented soy hides in many unsuspected items in your refrigerator and in your pantry such as ice cream, yogurt, pasta, and cereal. Common baking items that contain soy include flour. Why would flour have soy in it? The food industry puts soy in fortified flour so the label can boast more protein. Chocolate is often a place where you will find soy lecithin or if it's a liquid chocolate it may have soybean oil. Frostings often have soybean oil in them to make them more creamy and moist. Even sprinkles often have soy lecithin to keep them from sticking together and soybean oil to keep them moist.

Table 2: Food Items Possibly Containing Soy

Baby formula and food	Non-dairy desserts
Bacon	Pasta
Bagels	Protein bars
Bread	Protein powder
Burgers	Sauces
Cereal	Sausage
Cheese	Seasonings
Chocolates	Snack foods
Condiments	Soy sauce
Dressings	Tofu
Frozen foods	Turkey
Imitation foods	Vegetable oil
Margarines/spreads	Vegetable protein
Marinades	Waffles
Milk	Whipped toppings
Nuts and nut butter	Yogurt

Will The Food Label State If The Item Has Soy In It?

By law, food manufacturers are required to state on the labels if their product has soy in the ingredients. However, even when you don't think you are eating soy, you could be. For instance, eggs, though they do not exactly have soy directly added to them, may come from chickens that were fed soybean meal. Keep in mind, soy can also be a hidden addition to food and can hide under many aliases such as "textured vegetable protein" (TVP®), "vegetable oil", "lecithin", and "natural flavorings". In addition, soy is found in many health and beauty items. See Table 3 for a list of health and beauty items that may contain soy.

Table 3: Health and Beauty Items Possibly Containing Soy

Arthritis medications	Lotions
Bubble baths	Nail polish removers
Candles	Shampoos/Conditioners
Estrogen replacements	Soaps
Face and hand creams	Soft gel caps from lecithin

Do Non-Food Items Contain Soy?

For thousands of years, ancient farmers used soy as a fertilizer, not as food. It was also used industrially in a variety of ways, and in 1913 soy was actually listed in the United States Department of Agriculture (USDA) handbook not as a food, but as an industrial product. Today it is still used in many industrial applications, which is a much better place for soy rather than in our food supply. Soy is used to produce carpets, appliances, auto panels, building materials, tanks, and pipes. Soy is used in such items as adhesives, ink, lubricants, paint, plywood, plastics, and biodiesel fuel for cars and trucks. Some plastics known as urethanes are derived from soy. Soy is renewable, abundant, and biodegradable; hence it is preferred over petroleum products by many manufacturing companies.

Final Thoughts

There are many physicians, even some holistic doctors, advocating the use of soy in the diet and in supplements for treating menopausal symptoms or for promoting a healthy lifestyle. My (DB) clinical experience has clearly shown that these products are not the best available choices and can, in fact, be harmful. When you study the literature on soy, there is little use for non-fermented soy products and they should be avoided. The remaining chapters in this book will explain more about the soy deception. We believe a good place for soy is in ink for printing newspapers rather than in our food supply!

[1] Campbell, T. The Cornell-China Oxford Project on Nutrition, Health and Environment. 1990.

2

Fermented Versus Non-Fermented Soy

Introduction

Soy is promoted as a healthy food source by the soy industry. However, we have found soy to be an unhealthy food source, especially if it is non-fermented soy. To simplify, we will discuss soy in two groups: fermented or non-fermented. As previously stated, if we mention the word "soy", we are referring to non-fermented soy. Fermented soy will be referred to as such. Fermented soy is the way traditional Asian cultures ate and today continue to eat most of the soy in their diet.

Presently, soy is the cheapest crop to grow in the United States. It is less expensive for industry to use non-fermented versus fermented soy. Therefore, non-fermented soy has become a plentiful substance that has found its way into too many food products. Estimates are that over 50%-60% of supermarket food has soy as an ingredient. This chapter will discuss both fermented and non-fermented soy and teach you about which soy is less harmful for you (fermented soy) and which soy you should avoid (non-fermented soy).

It is important to read labels frequently to see if an item has soy in it because manufacturers often change the ingredients in packaged foods. Be wary when eating out at restaurants as many processed foods and fast foods have soy in them as filler. The best way to avoid soy is to prepare your own meals in your own kitchen. (See recipes in Chapter 9 to help guide you.)

Frequently Asked Questions

What Is Fermented Soy?

Fermented soy is produced by a host of bacteria, molds, and yeasts making it healthier for human consumption. Common fermented forms of soy include miso, natto, tempeh, and fermented soy sauce (e.g., shoyu or tamari). The fermentation of soy significantly reduces the anti-nutrient and anti-thyroid compounds such as trypsin inhibitor and phytic acid that are found in unfermented soy.

Fermenting soy creates health-promoting probiotics, the "good" bacteria, such as lactobacilli to enhance our intestinal health. Our bodies can utilize these bacteria to increase the availability, digestibility, and assimilation of nutrients as well as to maintain digestive and overall wellness.

Should I Eat Fermented Soy?

There is no easy 'yes' or 'no' answer here. The studies are contradictory on the health benefits of fermented soy. However, fermented soy is a better choice as compared to non-fermented soy. We feel small amounts of fermented soy products, used as condiments, such as miso, tempeh, natto, and fermented soy sauce (e.g., shoyu or tamari) can be part of a healthy diet. As previously mentioned, fermented soy was the traditional way that soy was used as in Asian diets. Fermented soy is still used in small dietary amounts by Asians. Keep in mind that Asian diets are <u>not</u> made up of soy milk, tofurky, and boca burgers!

Our experience has shown that fermented soy products, when used in small amounts, do not have the same negative influence on minerals, vitamins, and the thyroid that the non-fermented form of soy does. Natto, one form of fermented soy, is a very good source of Vitamin K2 that can help treat osteoporosis and bleeding disorders. I (DB) have used natto supplements successfully in my practice and find it a positive item for those suffering from osteoporosis.

How Is Soy Processed?

When soybeans are processed, every part of the bean is used for some particular purpose. First the soybeans are cleaned, then cracked, de-hulled, and finally rolled into flakes. This is when the soybean oil is extracted and then it, along with the rest of the bean, is put into our food supply or into animal feed.

Most soy goes through various forms of modern industrial processing methods as listed in Table 4. These methods are used to produce soybean oil, flour, and other soy byproducts contained in most processed foods. Soy flour and grits are used for baking, while soy hulls become cereals, breads, and animal feed. The soybean oil can be manufactured into margarines, spreads, dressings, and sauces.

Table 4: Soy Processing Methods

Adding chemicals
Bleaching
Boiling in petroleum-based solvents
Crushing into flakes
Deodorizing
Heat-blasting
Hydraulic or batch pressing
Solvent extraction
Washing in alkaline

What About Soy Milk?

Soy milk is produced when de-hulled soybeans are soaked in water, ground, and strained. The liquid that is left from straining is sweetened, flavoring is added as well as a stabilizer, and finally it is fortified with vitamins.

Soy milk is promoted by the soy industry as a healthy substitute for cow's milk. It is promoted to be used as milk for cereal, in shakes, or as a dairy alternative. However, we do not recommend ingesting any amount of soy milk, as it is not a "health" food. In fact, soy milk contains aluminum due to its manufacturing process. Furthermore, commercial soy milk is a non-fermented form of soy. It naturally contains little digestible calcium as it is bound to the bean's pulp, which makes it insoluble in humans. The calcium that is used to fortify soy milk is not a well absorbed form of calcium. Furthermore, soy milk (along with many rice and almond milks found in aseptic cartons) is often fortified with a plant-derived form of Vitamin D2 rather than a more bioavailable form of Vitamin D - Vitamin D3.

What About Soybean Oil?

Soybean oil has become the world's most widely used "edible" oil. According to the United Soybean Board 2009 Consumer Attitudes Report, consumers ranked soybean oil among the top three healthy oils. In the United States it is the most frequently consumed oil.

Soybean oil is used in shortening (e.g., Crisco®), spreads, and many cooking oils because it boasts that it is lower in saturated fat than animal fat or other cooking oils. It is used by the food industry in many items such as those listed in Table 5, as well as foods containing vegetable oil. Oil sold in the grocery store under the generic name of "vegetable oil" is usually 100 percent soy oil. For more on healthy oils and which oils we recommend cooking with see our book *The Guide to Healthy Eating, 2nd Edition*.

Table 5: Items that May Contain Soybean Oil

Bakery items	Processed foods
Canned foods	Salad dressing
Coffee creamer	Sauces
Cooking oil	Shortening
Margarine	Spreads
Mayonnaise	Vegetable oil

What About Soy Lecithin?

Soy lecithin, found in countless packaged foods, is actually a waste product left over after the soybean is processed. The primary source for commercial lecithin used to be egg lecithin, until the 1930s when it was found that soy lecithin could be recovered from the leftover sludge of soybean processing. The soy industry has managed to use every part of the soybean. Unfortunately, even the waste product soy lecithin has found its way into our food supply and is used as an additive in far too many foods.

Soy lecithin is used as a stabilizer in foods. In addition, it is used in bakery items to keep the dough from sticking and to improve its ability to rise. It helps give solidity in margarine and gives consistent texture to dressings and other creamy products. It is also used in chocolates and coatings and to counteract spattering during frying.

Soy lecithin is best known as an emulsifier which helps keep ingredients evenly mixed. It helps to add water to fatty or oily foods. The reason manufacturers want to add more water to food is because water has no calories or fat. Water can be used to replace some of the fat in foods such as hot dogs and salad dressings in order to place the "low fat" label on the finished product. Therefore, soy lecithin is usually found in foods that contain oil or water and foods that are low fat or low calorie. Table 6 lists some of the items that may contain soy lecithin.

Table 6: Items that May Contain Soy Lecithin

Baked goods	Instant mixes
Bread	Margarine
Cakes	Pharmaceuticals
Candy coatings	Pie crusts
Chocolate	Salad dressing
Chewing gum	Shortening
Ice cream	Waffles

What About Soy Protein Isolate?

Since 1959, soy protein has been added to many foods because of its properties of emulsification and texturizing. Far too many food products contain soy protein isolate. Table 7, page 42, lists a variety of foods that may have soy protein in them. Soy protein is increasing in popularity due to it being an inexpensive product and the false health claims perpetuated by the multibillion dollar soy industry.

Soy protein isolate is made in a factory where soy is mixed with an alkaline solution and subsequently acid washed in an aluminum tank. The process of acid washing in aluminum tanks results in high levels of aluminum found in many food products containing soy protein isolate. The resulting product is spray-dried at high temperatures to produce soy protein isolate. Soy protein isolate then can be converted into soy meats, and all the other soy-containing products readily available.[1]

Soy protein isolate and other forms of processed soy protein are added to animal feeds, protein shakes, as well as protein bars, and even soy infant formula. Isolates are used in meat products to improve texture and eating quality.

Besides elevated aluminum, there are other unhealthy agents in soy protein isolate. Nitrites, known carcinogens, are formed during the processing. Monosodium glutamate (MSG), a neurotoxin, is also formed during the processing of soy protein isolate. Furthermore, according to Kaayla Daniel, author of *The Whole Soy Story*, "Soy protein isolate was invented for use in cardboard; it hasn't actually been approved as a food ingredient."

Where Is Soy Protein Isolate Found?

One of the most common places you will see soy protein isolate as a nutritional substance is in protein powder. It is best to avoid these products. There are many brands of protein powders that do not contain soy protein isolate. Protein bars also frequently contain soy protein isolate and should be avoided.

Unfortunately, many supplements contain soy protein isolate. We believe that any nutritional company using soy protein isolate as an ingredient is doing a disservice to its clients. There are many nutritional companies in the marketplace not using soy protein isolate. Other items to be aware of that may also contain soy protein isolate are listed in Table 7.

Table 7: Items That May Contain Soy Protein

Baby foods	Infant formula
Baked goods	Imitation meats
Bakery mixes	Non-dairy foods
Beer and ale	Pasta
Beverage powders	Protein powders/bars
Cereals	Processed dairy
Cheese	Soups
Diet food products	Supplements
Frozen desserts	Vegetarian foods

What About Textured Soy Protein?

Another form of soy protein, known as textured soy protein (TSP) or textured vegetable protein (TVP®) is used as an ingredient of meat and dairy analogs. Hydrated TSP or TVP® is used often because of its resemblance to ground beef. It is often used as filler in various processed foods and as a ground beef replacement to make vegetarian or vegan versions of traditional meat dishes such as chili, spaghetti, sloppy joes, tacos, and burritos. Additionally, it is sometimes added to meat such as burgers, sausages, franks, and cold cuts. Sadly, it is very popular in school cafeterias, hospitals, and prisons as a filler to help cut the cost of such items as hamburger. It is enticing to institutions with its very low cost (at less than a third of the price of ground beef) and its relatively long shelf life.

Final Thoughts

It is best to avoid non-fermented soy products in your diet. This includes soy protein, soybean oil, soy flour, and soy milk. The ingestion of large amounts of non-fermented soy products may lead to many health problems including thyroid and hormonal imbalances as well as cancer. These issues are discussed in later chapters of this book.

If you want to use soy in your diet, experiment with adding small amounts of the fermented forms of soy such as natto, miso, tempeh, shoyu. Instead of soy milk, try coconut milk as a dairy alternative in your oatmeal or smoothies!

[1] Adapted from The Dark Side of Soy by Mary Enig and Sally Fallon. Nexus Magazine. VOL 7, N.3 (April-May 2000).

3

Why Avoid Soy?

Introduction

Soy can now be found in countless products at the grocery store and is touted to be the ultimate health food. It is commonly used as a substitute for meat and milk. Media and industry hype would have you believe that good health is associated with a high soy intake. The annual U.S. consumer attitude surveys by the United Soybean Board stated that 85% of those polled in 2008 rated soy products as "healthy," a significant increase from the 59% who in 1997 thought this was the case. Moreover, according to the Soyfoods Association of North America, from 1992 to 2006 soy food sales increased from $300 million to nearly $4 billion.

Why has the perception of soy changed so dramatically? Deceptive advertising has allowed the soy industry to change the perception of soy in order for soy to be considered a health food. The soy industry has managed to stake their claim that soy can help nearly every condition including improving and preventing heart disease, alleviating symptoms associated with menopause, reducing the risk of certain cancers, as well as lowering levels of "bad" cholesterol or LDL-cholesterol.

What would you say if you found out soy was not the "health food" it has been portrayed to be? What would you say if the ingestion of soy has been shown to cause nutritional deficiencies, hormonal imbalances, infertility, and other diseases?

The positive side of soy is far overshadowed by the negative aspects and we suggest you avoid it or strictly limit your consumption of it. This includes the most popular forms of soy such as the highly processed, non-fermented soy commonly found in soy burgers, soy cheese, soy milks, etc.

Frequently Asked Questions

Is Soy A Health Food?

No, soy (non-fermented soy) is not a health food. Many claims about soy state that it offers many health benefits. These statements claim that soy is a good source of protein but low in saturated fats and cholesterol. Other claims state that soy ingestion promotes lower rates of heart disease, as well as breast and other cancers, fewer menopause symptoms, and healthier bones. However, there are many other studies supporting the fact that soy may not be the "health food" it has been proclaimed to be and may actually contain many harmful components. Soy, in fact, is listed as poisonous in the U.S. Food and Drug Administration Poisonous Plant Database.[1] Our experience has clearly shown that patients who ingest a large amount of soy have more health issues as compared to those that do not eat it. (Note: I (DB) have clearly found that those patients who ingest large quantities of non-fermented soy have more health problems as compared to patients who avoid it).

What Are The Problems With Soy?

There are many concerns with soy; it contains many anti-nutrients and components that are toxic to humans. The ingestion of soy has also been linked to the development of many health issues such as breast cancer, digestive issues, hypothyroidism, infertility, thyroid cancer, and many other disorders as listed in Table 8, page 58.

There are many potential problems with soy. The potential adverse effects of soy include:

1) Soy causes many thyroid problems. It is a known goitrogen—it promotes goiter or swelling of the thyroid gland. (More about this in Chapter 5.)

2) Soy inhibits the uptake of iodine, which is used by the thyroid gland in the production of thyroid hormones. (More about this in Chapter 5.)

3) Soy contains phytoestrogens (plant estrogens) which may disrupt endocrine function. (More about this in Chapter 4.)

4) Soy contains large amounts of phytates (including phytic acid). Phytic acid is the storage form of phosphate in plants. Research has shown that phytic acid has been found to reduce the assimilation of minerals including calcium, copper, iron, magnesium, and zinc. The fermentation process helps in neutralizing phytic acid, which is one reason why fermented soy is healthier for you.

5) Soy has also been shown to increase the body's requirements for vitamin D.

6) It has long been recognized that soy consumption can cause vitamin B12 deficiency.

7) During the processing of soy, highly carcinogenic nitrates and a toxin called lysinoalanine are formed. Also, many soy foods often contain MSG and aluminum.

8) Most soy in the United States is genetically modified (GM). It is estimated that about half of the American soybean crop planted in 1999 carries a gene that makes it resistant to an herbicide (Roundup®) used to control weeds. Therefore, these GM soy plants are continually sprayed with large amounts of Roundup®. (More about GM soy can be found in Chapter 8.)

9) Soy has one of the highest percentages of pesticide contamination of any food.

10) Soy is highly allergenic and is in fact one of the top eight food allergens. It is found as filler in so many foods that people with allergies may be at risk. (More about soy and allergies can be found in Chapter 7.)

11) Soy contains saponins which have been show to damage the mucosal lining of the intestine or cause leaky gut. (More about leaky gut can be found in Chapter 7.)

12) Soy contains oxalates which can prevent calcium absorption and have been linked to the development of kidney stones.

What About Phytic Acid In Soy?

Phytic acid is considered an anti-nutritional component of cereals, nuts, seeds, legumes, and grains. Soy belongs to the family of legumes. Other members of the legume family include beans - such as adzuki, navy, red kidney, etc., as well as chickpeas. Peanuts are also technically a legume, not a nut. Soy actually contains one of the highest amounts of phytic acid as compared to most other grains and legumes. In many cases, phytic acid can be neutralized by soaking, cooking, or sprouting. However, with the soybean, this is not the case.

Phytates are substances that can block the body's uptake of minerals - calcium, copper, iron, magnesium, and zinc in the intestinal tract.[2][3] Ingesting food with high phytic acid content, including soy, may lead to deficiencies of these minerals. This is a particular issue for young growing children because it may cause growth problems and is one major reason why a child's diet should not be based on soy products and soy milk.

The only way to neutralize the phytic acid in soy is through fermentation methods. This is one of the reasons fermented soy is a healthier choice (in small amounts) if you are going to eat soy in your diet.

What About The Protease-Inhibitors In Soy?

Proteases are important enzymes that are used to break protein down into amino acids which are used to build muscles and other tissues. A protease inhibitor such as trypsin, deactivates the action of proteases and may disrupt protein digestion. Animals given these inhibitors have been found to develop problems with the pancreas and cancer.

Soy is one of the most potent trypsin inhibitors known. Trypsin is an enzyme that has important functions in the body. Dr. Nicholas Gonzales, one of the world's foremost researchers on the use of enzymes to treat pancreatic cancer believes that soy "...is the most powerful trypsin inhibitor of any food on earth."[4] Trypsin is a pancreatic enzyme that Dr. Gonzales has found very helpful for treating pancreatic cancer. Fermented soy, however, is virtually free of protease inhibitors.

What Nutrient Deficiencies Are Associated With Soy Intake?

Soy has been associated with vitamins B12 and D deficiencies. My (DB) clinical experience has shown that those patients who ingest the largest amounts of soy often have the lowest levels of vitamin B12. Soy milk manufacturers have recognized the problems in their products and now add in some of the vitamins and minerals that soy actually depletes in the body. For example, many soy milk companies add in vitamin D2, the synthetic version of vitamin D3. Synthetic D2 is not as helpful for your body as natural D3. You should avoid all supplements and products that contain synthetic vitamins such as vitamin D2.

What Heavy Metals Are In Soy?

Soy products often have high levels of the heavy metal aluminum in them. There is a two-fold reason for this – the first involves the soil where soy is grown and the amount of aluminum transferred from the soil to the soybean. The second reason is that aluminum tanks are used for the acid wash processing. The aluminum can leach into the final soy product. In addition, the storage containers in the factories are aluminum. Aluminum has been associated with kidney and nervous system disorders.

What About Soy And Gas Or Other Digestive Disturbances?

Soy eaters often find they suffer from excess gas and bloating. The oligosaccharides (sugars) present in soy can create increased gas production. However, fermentation seems to decrease the flatulence factor in soy.

Soy also contains photochemicals known as saponins that may lead to gastrointestinal difficulties and leaky gut as well as causing diarrhea and bloating. Digestive disturbances and excess gas may also be symptoms of a soy allergy or sensitivity. Other symptoms of an allergy to soy include sneezing, runny nose, hives, shortness of breath, or more seriously, anaphylactic shock. More on soy allergies can be found in Chapter 7.

What About Soy And Oxalates?

Soy is high in oxalates, which have been known to disrupt calcium absorption and can lead to calcium deficiencies as well as kidney stones. The American Dietetic Association (ADA) suggests that patients with calcium oxalate kidney stones limit oxalate levels to no more than 10 milligrams per serving. Many foods that contain soy and soy derivatives (e.g., textured soy protein, soy protein isolate) far exceed this level. Texturized soy protein for example has 638 milligrams of oxalate in an average three ounce serving! It is important to be extra cautious about ingesting soy if you have history of kidney stones.

What Health Issues May Be Associated With Soy Intake?

Although the soy industry would like you to believe soy can help with everything from menopausal symptoms and slowing or reversing osteoporosis to cancer prevention, the fact is most soy on the market is not a health food; in fact it is an unhealthy food. Non-fermented soy has been associated with many diseases and health issues. Table 8 lists just some of the common issues that have been linked to soy consumption.

Table 8: Health Issues Associated With Soy

Allergies	Infertility
Birth defects	Kidney stones
Cancer	Malnutrition
Cognitive decline	Reproductive disorders
Digestive distress	Thyroid dysfunction
Heart disease	Weight gain

Final Thoughts

Soy manufacturers would like you to believe that soy is a health food. Nothing could be further from the truth. The ingestion of non-fermented soy products leads to nutritional imbalances, digestive disorders, hormone problems, and thyroid issues. For optimal health, we recommend avoiding non-fermented soy in the form of soy protein isolate, soybean oil, and soy flour, as well as soy meat and milk products.

[1] U.S. Food and Drug Administration.
http://www.accessdata.fda.gov/scripts/plantox/detail.cfm?id=16372

[2] Am. J. Clin. Nut. 56. NO.3. 1992.573-8

[3] Am. J. Clin.Nut. 48. No. 5. 1988;1301-6

[4] From Townsend Letter. 301/302. Pg. 86. Aug/Sept. 2008

4

Soy and Phytoestrogens

Introduction

Many women have been convinced they are improving their health by eating soy. The soy manufacturers (as well as the media), through slick advertising, have brainwashed women to believe that ingesting soy is healthy. Furthermore, the powers-that-be claim that soy's phytoestrogens are the miracle nutrients we have all been waiting for. The soy proponents would have women believe that soy phytoestrogens mimic estrogen and tout them to be safe and helpful for relieving menopausal symptoms, as well as improving osteoporosis, and even treating and preventing cancer.

However, many other studies show soy phytoestrogens disrupt thyroid and other endocrine functions, decrease fertility, and can cause cancer. As will be discussed in Chapter 6, infants ingesting soy formula are actually being exposed to a similar amount of hormone that is found in several birth control pills. Needless to say, we do not recommend exposing your baby to the hormonal chemicals found in soy formula. We believe you should exercise great caution with any product that can mimic estrogen function or disrupt hormone function.

Many items that disrupt proper hormone functioning can be classified as endocrine disrupters. These items will cause unwanted results in the long run. Furthermore, endocrine disrupters are not healthy items; they should be avoided. We can assure you that soy is not the safe product that soy proponents have deceptively promoted them to be.

Frequently Asked Questions

What Are Phytoestrogens?

Phytoestrogens are a group of chemicals that resemble estrogen molecules. These items mimic the hormone estrogen. Estrogen is a necessary hormone for childbearing, as well as for bone and heart health in women. Phytoestrogens can enhance or disrupt the natural estrogens produced in the human body. It is best to take a cautious approach to phytoestrogens as they can often yield unpredictable results and can disrupt endocrine function. This can result in many serious problems including causing cancer.

Are The Phytoestrogens In Soy Safe?

The answer to the above question is unequivocally "No." Soy has been found to have abnormal effects on the hormonal system of both males and females. It can also be very damaging to the reproductive system. Furthermore, phytoestrogens disrupt thyroid function as discussed further in Chapter 5. The most notable of phytoestrogens is a group of substances known as isoflavones that are found abundantly in soy. The primary soy isoflavones are genistein and daidzein. As will be discussed in Chapter 5, these isoflavones have been shown to disrupt the normal functioning of the thyroid gland. Though isoflavones are touted to prevent cancer, coronary heart disease, and osteoporosis, other researchers have reached opposite conclusions. For example, genistein and daidzein have been found to be carcinogenic and DNA-damaging.[2] We feel there is no indication to eat any foods or to take any supplements containing genistein and daidzein.

Does Soy Help Menopausal Symptoms In Women?

There is no question that the phytoestrogen component of soy may improve the menopausal symptoms that women frequently suffer. This includes hot flashes, mood swings, depression, and anxiety. Although soy may help improve the symptoms of menopause, we feel the adverse effects of soy do not warrant its use for treating menopause. We feel there are much safer and better substances available to treat menopausal symptoms including eating a healthy diet as well as supplementing with bioidentical, natural hormones.

One of the first things we tell our patients who are suffering from menopausal symptoms is to improve their eating habits. This means eating good fats as well as ingesting a whole food diet. Removing the "whites" – white sugar, flour, and salt – helps treat the symptoms of menopause. Furthermore, drinking adequate amounts of pure water will also aid menopausal symptoms.

Our experience has shown that taking Vitamin E (mixed tocopherols) from 400-1,000 I.U. at bedtime can relieve the nighttime hot flashes and insomnia that accompany menopausal symptoms.

There can be no faster relief from menopausal symptoms than the use of bioidentical hormones. If you are suffering from menopausal symptoms, we suggest having your hormone levels checked, including estrogen, progesterone, and testosterone (both free testosterone and total testosterone). From this information, you can ascertain where things are imbalanced. Finding a health care provider knowledgeable in prescribing bioidentical natural hormones is a starting point (www.acam.org or the Broda O. Barnes, M.D. Research Foundation, Inc., 203.261.2101). I (DB) frequently prescribe combinations of bioidentical natural progesterone, estradiol, estriol, and testosterone to help my patients restore hormonal balance. For more information on bioidentical, natural hormones, please read **The Miracle of Natural Hormones, 2nd Edition**.

Does Soy Destroy Libido In Men?

Soy has been known to decrease fertility in many different animal species. This includes cows, sheep, rabbits, cheetahs, guinea pigs, birds, and mice.[2] My (DB) clinical experience has continually shown that soy use in men is a major cause of low libido. We tell our male patients that it is impossible to improve their libido if they are ingesting non-fermented soy products. For hundreds of years, monks have been known to use soy as a way to lower their libido.

The large amounts of phytoestrogens in soy are responsible for lowering the libido in men. A newborn male experiences testosterone surges after birth. There can be negative consequences to having a newborn male ingest soy formula, which contains a large amount of phytoestrogens.

Does Soy Prevent Osteoporosis?

The soy industry would love for us to believe that soy can prevent and treat osteoporosis. The soy industry constantly reminds us that Asian cultures have less osteoporosis as compared to Western societies. There are positive studies showing that soy improves bone density and results in fewer fractures and there are negative studies that fail to show a benefit. Most of the positive studies point to increased bone mass on a bone mineral density test with the use of soy. Unfortunately, solely relying on bone mineral density is a poor way to assess one's risk for osteoporosis. Asians typically have a lowered bone mineral density as compared to Western women, yet have lower rates of fractures. More information about this paradox can be found in **Drugs That Don't Work and Natural Therapies That Do, 2nd Edition**.

Soy has also been shown to increase the body's need for vitamin D. Furthermore, it has long been recognized that soy consumption can cause vitamin B12 deficiency. Both vitamins B12 and D are necessary to prevent and treat osteoporosis. Our clinical experience has shown that those patients who ingest the largest amounts of soy often have the lowest levels of vitamins B12 and D.

It is interesting that the soy industry can promote soy as a healthy way to prevent or treat osteoporosis when soy has been shown to deplete the body of many of the vital minerals and vitamins necessary to maintain optimal bone structure and function.

Does Soy Effect Fertility?

Yes, and unfortunately not in a positive way. Studies have long shown a connection with soy and infertility in animals, and evidence is rising for this same negative impact in humans. Soy formula has been shown to put infants at risk for future reproductive problems. Moreover, both men and women with higher intake of soy and soy isoflavones may have issues with infertility. Harvard University researchers reported that eating half a serving of soy per day lowers sperm concentrations and may play a role in male infertility, particularly in obese men.[3]

What About Hormone Sensitive Cancers?

We have an epidemic of breast and prostate cancer in the U.S. Presently, women in the U.S. have a one in seven chance of getting breast cancer. One in three men are suffering with prostate cancer. There are epidemic rates of other hormone-sensitive cancers occurring (including uterine and ovarian cancer). Animal studies have shown that the estrogen-like isoflavone, genestein (found in soy), when given to pregnant rats could cause increased changes leading to breast cancer in the offspring.

Final Thoughts

Soy should not be used for treating menopausal symptoms. Its use has been shown to cause thyroid disorders and nutritional imbalances as discussed in other chapters. Soy can also inhibit a man's libido. (Note: I (DB) have observed in my practice more hormonal imbalances in women and men who ingest soy.) Furthermore, how the soy industry can promote soy as a positive treatment for osteoporosis is beyond us. Any substance that depletes vital minerals and vitamins will not help or treat osteoporosis. Non-fermented soy is not a health food; not only should it be avoided, it should be pulled from the marketplace.

[2] *True Health, the magazine of Carotec Inc.*, Naples, Florida. May/June 2004.

[2] *Mothering.* Issue 124. May/June 2004

[3] *Hum. Reprod.* (2008) 23(11): 2584-2590

5

Soy and the Thyroid

Introduction

As you have read in the previous chapters, non-fermented soy products are not healthy products for anyone to ingest. The use of excessive non-fermented soy items in the diet including soy milk, soy hot dogs, vegetarian burgers, tofu, and soy cheeses, result in a host of mineral, vitamin, and hormonal imbalances.

Besides all of the nutritional deficiencies caused by soy, one of the most distressing adverse effects of soy food is that it can cause thyroid problems. Soy is a known goitrogen. A goitrogen causes abnormal swelling of the thyroid gland. Furthermore, soy acts as a powerful anti-thyroid agent as well as a hormone disrupter. This chapter will review the interaction of between soy and the thyroid gland.

When I (DB) started studying and utilizing holistic medicine nearly 20 years ago, I was stunned at the number of patients suffering from thyroid problems. There are estimates that up to 40% or more of the U.S. population may be suffering from an undiagnosed thyroid condition. Thyroid diseases, from hypothyroidism to autoimmune thyroid illnesses as well as thyroid cancer are occurring at pandemic to epidemic rates. Why has this occurred? One of the main reasons why we are seeing such an epidemic of thyroid disorders is due to soy consumption as well as iodine deficiency. Iodine deficiency will be discussed later in this chapter.

Frequently Asked Questions

What Is The Thyroid?

The thyroid is a butterfly-shaped gland located in the lower part of the neck. Though it weighs less than an ounce, the thyroid is responsible for many critical functions in the body. It is one of the largest endocrine glands in the body. Our muscles, organs, and cells all depend on the thyroid hormones, the principal ones being triiodothyronine (T_3) and thyroxine (T_4), to properly function. The thyroid gland also interacts with the other endocrine glands of the body such as the adrenal glands. A properly functioning thyroid gland will help the other glands function optimally. Thyroid hormone influences all of the body processes such as growth, development, reproduction, and metabolism.

What Thyroid Disorders Are Related To Soy Consumption?

Soy consumption can lead to a variety of thyroid disorders including auto-immune conditions (i.e., Graves' or Hashimoto's), goiter, hypothyroidism, hyperthyroidism, thyroid nodules, and even thyroid cancer.

How Does Soy Inhibit Thyroid Function?

The medical research is clear: over 75 years of studies have shown that soy adversely affects thyroid function. The isoflavones in soy are capable of blocking the conversion of inactive (T_4) thyroid hormone to active (T_3) thyroid hormone. In other words, it can cause or worsen thyroid disorders and its use can result in hypothyroidism. (See Table 11, page 83 for a list of symptoms associated with hypothyroidism). In addition, researchers have identified the isoflavones in soy as goitrogens – endocrine disrupters and substances that cause goiter. In other words, they cause swelling of the thyroid gland. In fact, researchers have reported that infants developed goiter and hypothyroidism due to the ingestion of soy formula.[1] [2] Furthermore, soy formula has been associated with the development of autoimmune thyroid disorder. A case control study found children with autoimmune thyroid disease received significantly more soy formula as compared to their non-affected siblings.[3] See Chapter 6 for more about the downfalls of soy formula.

What About Soy Isoflavones?

Soy has been shown to contain compounds called isoflavones. Isoflavones are chemicals in the flavonoid or bioflavonoid family and are known for being goitrogenic, disrupting the hormonal system, and acting as an anti-thyroid agent. Soy isoflavones have been shown to reduce thyroid hormone absorption and interfere with thyroid hormone action.[4] Isoflavones inhibit an important thyroid substance known as thyroid peroxidase.[5] Thyroid peroxidase is necessary for the thyroid gland to use iodine to make thyroid hormone. Soy's primary isoflavones that block this important reaction are known as daidzein and genistein. Daidzein and genistein are found in large amounts in soy products and some nutritional supplements. In fact, genistein is a more powerful inhibitor of thyroid peroxidase then many anti-thyroid drugs. We feel you should avoid any supplement that contains either genistein or daidzein.

What About Goitrogens In Soy?

Goitrogens that interfere with thyroid function are naturally occurring in many foods common in our diet. Aside from soy, goitrogens can be found in cruciferous vegetables and other foods listed in Table 9. These can be neutralized by regular cooking methods. Soy however, is different in that the goitrogens are not easily deactivated or neutralized. Soy should be eaten sparingly and it is important to ensure adequate iodine supplementation to counter soy's goitrogenic effects.

Table 9: Goitrogenic Foods

Broccoli	Millet
Brussels sprouts	Peaches
Cabbage	Peanuts
Cauliflower	Pine nuts
Cassava	Radishes
Kale	
Kohlrabi	Soybean and soy products, including tofu
Mustard	
Rutabaga	Spinach
Turnips	Strawberries

What About Iodine And Soy Consumption?

It is important to point out that when iodine deficiency is present, the problems with soy, and particularly the isoflavones daidzein and genistein, are accentuated. Researchers have reported that rats fed a defatted soy bean diet (similar to the low fat soy products available to humans) had a 200% increase in goiter compared to rats not fed soy. Iodine deficient rats fed a soy diet had a 1000% increase in goiter compared to rats not fed soy.[6]

Iodine deficiency is occurring in the vast majority of Americans. In fact, my (DB) research has shown a vast majority of people are iodine deficient. Iodine is a necessary ingredient for the formation of all of the thyroid hormones. Correcting an iodine deficiency problem can make dramatic positive changes in one's health status. For more information on iodine, please read ***Iodine Why You Need It, Why You Can't Live Without It, 4th Edition***.

Is Any Amount Of Soy Safe For Thyroid Function?

Fermented soy does not seem to cause the thyroid problems that non-fermented soy causes and is not often ingested in quantities as large as non-fermented items like soy milk. As previously mentioned, we suggest that you avoid non-fermented soy in any form. Especially for infants and children – no amount is recommended. Only a small amount of soy is required to cause problems with the thyroid. According to the Soy Online Service a mere 30 mg/day of soy isoflavones can have a negative impact on thyroid function. There are 30 mg of soy isoflavones in just 5-8 ounces of soy milk. We recommend viewing the online USDA listing of the isoflavone content of common foods to help you determine what foods you should eat and what foods you may want to avoid in your diet at: http://www.nal.usda.gov/fnic/foodcomp/Data/isoflav/isoflav.html

How Do I Know If I Have A Thyroid Disorder?

Thyroid disorders plague America and often go undiagnosed in many people. The Colorado Thyroid Disease Prevalence Study estimated that the rate of hypothyroidism in the general population was approximately 10%.[7] My (DB) experience has clearly shown that the number of people suffering from thyroid disorders is much higher—in the range of 40-60%. More information about this can be found in ***Overcoming Thyroid Disorders, 2nd Edition***.

Tables 10 and 11 list some of the common symptoms associated with thyroid disorders, particularly hyperthyroid and hypothyroid. The conventional approach to diagnosing thyroid problems relies on blood tests. However, we believe relying solely on the blood tests will ensure that many (millions) patients suffering from thyroid problems will be missed. In order to reliably identify thyroid conditions, we recommend finding a qualified health care practitioner who is knowledgeable about a holistic approach to diagnosis. This should include not only blood tests, but also basal body temperature, as well as a complete history and physical exam. For more on thyroid disorders, we refer you to **Overcoming Thyroid Disorders, 2nd Edition.**

Table 10: Symptoms of Hyperthyroidism
(An overactive thyroid)

Fatigue	Menstrual disturbance
Goiter	Nervousness
Heat intolerance	Palpitations
Hyperactivity	Thinning of skin
Hypertension	Tremor
Irritability	Weakness
Increase perspiration	Weight loss

> **Table 11: Symptoms of Hypothyroidism**
> **(An underactive thyroid)**
>
> Brittle nails
> Cold hands/feet
> Constipation
> Fatigue, exhaustion
> Feeling rundown and sluggish
> Depression
> Difficulty concentrating, brain fog
> Dry, coarse, and/or itchy skin
> Dry, coarse, and/or thinning hair
> Elevated cholesterol
> Feeling cold, especially in the extremities
> Increased or disrupted menstrual flow
> Infertility/miscarriage
> Muscle cramps
> Poor eyebrow growth
> Puffy eyes
> Unexplained or excessive weight gain

Final Thoughts

The current promotion of soy by the powers-that-be and the subsequent increase of soy in the American diet has not led to better health in our society. In fact, it is partially responsible for the epidemic rise in thyroid disorders. Our experience has clearly shown that patients who ingest a lot of non-fermented soy products suffer from thyroid problems and other hormonal issues, as well as nutritional imbalances. Particularly at risk are those patients with iodine deficiency. My (DB) research has shown over 95% of patients are suffering from iodine deficiency. Others at risk are those using isoflavone supplements, vegans who use soy as a principle meat or dairy alternative, or those who were or are being fed soy infant formula.

We believe more and more people will have thyroid issues as soy consumption increases in the population. To ensure optimal thyroid function, it is best to avoid soy.

[1] Pediatrics. 24:752-760. 1959

[2] N. Eng. J. of Med. 262:351-3. 1960

[3] J. Am. Coll. Nutr. 9:164-7. 1990

[4] Thyroid. 16:249-258. 2006

[5] Biochem. Pharm. Vol. 54. 1997. 1087-96

[6] Carcinogenesis 2000. Apr. 21(4)

[7] Canaris, Gay, et al. The Colorado Thyroid Disease Prevalence Study. Arch Intern. Med. Vol 160, Feb 28, 2000

6

Soy Formula

Introduction

Proper nutrition is crucial to ensure an infant has optimal body and brain growth, development and function, as well as all-around good health. There is no question that the best food for a newborn is the milk from the mother. In Western societies, many women cannot or will not breast feed. Infants are typically fed a cow's-milk based formula product. If there is any sign of problems in the infant such as an allergy or gastrointestinal upset, the mother is often advised by her health care provider to change the formula. Usually, the advice is to change to a soy-based formula.

Soy formula should be avoided at all costs as it is not a healthy formula for a newborn. Soy is associated with thyroid abnormalities, immune system dysfunction, hormonal problems, and digestive complaints.

This section will inform you more about why we not only disagree with the advice to use soy formula as a dairy formula alternative, but why we also feel that soy-based formulas should be removed from the market altogether.

Frequently Asked Questions

Is Soy Formula A Good Choice For Infants?

The quick and easy answer to the above question is "no". Soy formula, when it first came on the market, was actually promoted as healthier than breast milk. This promotion was an outright lie. In fact, although the FDA proclaims soy infant formula as safe, The Israeli Health Ministry and other government bodies have all issued warnings about soy formula. The Israeli Health Ministry, for example, has recommended that the consumption of soy foods be limited for young children and adults and that soy formula should be avoided altogether by infants. If the FDA was working for us, the U.S. citizens, they would issue similar proclamations.

Why Do Doctors Recommend Soy Formula?

The most common reason that doctors recommend soy formula is due to dairy allergies, lactose intolerance, or digestive complaints in an infant. The American Academy of Pediatrics estimates about 25% of infants in the United States are on soy formula. The approximate size of the soy infant formula market has doubled in the last 10 years and is estimated to bring in revenue of $750 million out of the $3 billion infant formula market. Despite all the advertising and big dollars behind this market, parents need to know the truth – soy formula is one of the worst food choices they can make for their infant. Parents also need to be aware that a soy allergy is almost as common (or more common) as a cow's milk allergy. More about soy and allergies can be found in Chapter 7. Although it's promoted to be a great alternative, soy formula can actually cause more serious health issues.

What Are The Dangers Of Soy Formula?

There are many dangers with soy formula. First of all, soy formula often contains soy protein isolate. As mentioned in Chapter 2, soy protein isolate is associated with many negative health issues including hypothyroidism. In addition, soy protein isolate is extracted from soy using high temperatures and caustic chemicals, which leaves carcinogens in the end product.

Soy formula unfortunately also contains other negative items such as phytates, phytoestrogens, protease inhibitors, lectins, allergenic proteins, aluminum, and manganese.

Furthermore, other ingredients often found in soy formula include unlisted ingredients (certainly not found in mother's breast milk) such as: carrageenan, guar gum, sodium hydroxide (caustic soda), potassium citrate monohydrate, tricalcium phosphate, dibasic magnesium phosphate trihydrate, BHA, and BHT.

Soy formula is lacking in many essential ingredients found in mother's milk. This includes linoleic and oleic essential fatty acids, DHA, lactoferrin, immune factors, T-cells, B-cells, and interferon. Finally, soy formula does not have cholesterol which is a key component of breast milk and essential in the proper development of a newborn's brain and nervous system.

What About The Phytoestrogens In Soy Formula?

One of the most dangerous problems with soy formula is the phytoestrogens. Phytoestrogens are estrogen-like products commonly found in soy and soy-derived items. In soy, the phytoestrogens are known as isoflavones (e.g., genistein and daidzein). Isoflavones, being similar in structure to our own endogenously-produced estrogens, can interfere with the action of our native estrogens.

In 1997, researchers reported that infants fed soy formula ingested a whopping 28-47mg of isoflavones—estrogen-like compounds found in soy.[1] The author of this study concluded, "The daily exposure of infants to isoflavones in soy infant formulas is 6–11 fold higher on a bodyweight basis than the same dose in adults." Furthermore, researchers found that circulating concentrations of isoflavones in seven infants fed soy-based formula were 13,000–22,000 times higher than the expected plasma estradiol concentrations. This amount of estrogen was reported to "...be sufficient to exert biological effects, whereas the contribution of isoflavones from breast-milk and cow-milk is negligible."

Researchers have estimated that an infant exclusively fed soy formula received the estrogen equivalent of five birth control pills per day.[2] This, alone, is enough evidence to prove that feeding soy formula to a newborn baby or an infant does not make biochemical, hormonal, or common sense. More on the phytoestrogens in soy can be found in Chapter 4.

What About Soy Formula And Thyroid Function?

The previously mentioned isoflavones (e.g., genistein and daidzein) have been shown to be anti-thyroid agents or goitrogenic (i.e., can cause goiter or an enlarged thyroid gland). These chemicals inhibit the conversion from inactive to active thyroid hormone and furthermore inhibit the organifying effects of iodine in the thyroid gland. The end result is that soy ingestion in children will cause an increased risk of thyroid problems and put children at risk of abnormal growth and development. Soy formula feeding to infants has also been correlated with autoimmune thyroid conditions later in life.[3] More information on how soy impacts thyroid conditions can be found in Chapter 5.

Does Soy Formula Contain Excessive Manganese?

Soy milk formula contains excessive amounts of manganese at about 200-300 ug/l as compared to breast milk at 4-6 ug/l and cow's milk formula at 30-50 ug/l.[4] A baby's growing immune system and liver cannot handle this excess overload. Moreover, the growing brain is vulnerable and exposure to toxic substances can have long term negative effects. High levels of manganese have been linked to ADD/ADHD, brain damage, and other behavioral disorders in children.

Does Soy Formula Contain Excessive Aluminum?

Soy formula has been shown to have ten times more aluminum as milk-based formula and one hundred times as much as breast milk. The aluminum is present due to the soy plants ability to absorb aluminum from the soil. Furthermore, due to ingredients used in the making of soy formula and the processing – in aluminum vats – aluminum is further concentrated in the end product. Aluminum can have a toxic effect on the kidneys and the nervous system and can be especially detrimental to a newborn baby and a growing child.

In the 2008 journal, "Pediatrics," (the journal of the American Academy of Pediatrics) researchers reported, "….aluminum content of human milk is 4 to 65ng/mL, that of soy protein-based formula is 600 to 1300ng/mL. The toxicity of aluminum is traced to increased deposition in bone and in the central nervous system."[5]

What About Early Puberty Development In Girls?

Over the last 30 years, young girls are developing secondary sexual characteristics at a much earlier age. There is no question that the age of puberty—when young girls begin to menstruate and develop has declined over the last 20 years. One percent of girls show signs of breast development before age three. A study in 1997 determined that by eight years of age, 8 percent of Caucasian girls and nearly 25 percent of African American girls show signs of early pubertal development.[6] A recent Dutch study found girls starting to develop puberty over one year earlier as compared to fifteen years ago.

As compared to other children, larger numbers of African American children use soy formula. As Kaayla Daniels, author of *The Whole Soy Story*, states, "Because of perceived or real lactose intolerance, African American babies are much more likely to receive soy formula" as compared to Caucasian babies.[7] In Puerto Rico, researchers found soy infant feeding was associated with early puberty signs in girls.[8] This early pubertal development in girls is the direct result of the environmental estrogens and increased soy use, which are so ubiquitous in the environment. These products contain chemicals called "xeno-estrogens" or estrogen mimics. They are found in a variety of consumer products including plastics, pesticides, animal foods, and soy.

What About Soy Formula For Boys?

Soy formula is not a healthy choice for young girls or boys. We believe that newborn boys should not be given soy formula. The excess amount of phytoestrogens found in soy is bound to cause problems and has been linked to puberty delay in boys. It is thought that the phytoestrogens in soy can disrupt the normal function of testosterone in a young boy.[9] Estrogens occupying those sites can be detrimental to the programming for later sexual development that occurs during that precious time.

There has also been an epidemic of genital problems in newborn males over the last 20 years. Hypospadias, a condition which is a birth defect of the urethra in males, has increased 200% over the last 20 years. Researchers have reported that boys born to mothers who maintained a vegetarian diet had a greater exposure to estrogen-like chemicals. It is common for those eating a vegetarian diet to ingest more soy than those that eat an omnivore diet. Sperm counts in males have been falling for the last 30 years. Testicular cancer has been rising. All of these problems in males may be related to the excess exposure to the environmental estrogens including the estrogen-like chemicals in soy.

What If You Don't Want To Give Your Infant Cow's Milk Formula?

All mothers want the best health for their child. Many people turn to soy formula because they think it is a healthier choice than typical cow's milk formula. Or they may choose it for moral reasons, such as vegetarianism. Soy marketing has convinced mothers that soy formula is a better choice or a good alternative to cow's milk formula. However, thankfully, there are other options. If you cannot breastfeed or for other reasons are looking for alternatives including non-milk alternatives, please refer to www.westonaprice.org for information on homemade formulas and alternatives for feeding babies.

What If Your Child Is Allergic To Cow's Milk Formula?

Soy formula has been promoted as a complete protein without the allergenic effect of cow's milk. Hence, many infants diagnosed with a dairy allergy are given soy as the substitute of choice. Unfortunately, parents have not been given the whole truth about soy. In fact, in studies soy has shown to be just as allergenic or even more allergenic as compared to cow's milk. Symptoms of soy allergy are similar to those of milk allergies including sinus and ear infections, crankiness, joint paint, and fatigue, or stomach pain. Additionally, the pitfalls of soy far outweigh any benefits that may come from ingesting it. More on soy and allergies can be found in Chapter 7.

Final Thoughts

Would you knowingly feed your infant birth control pills? All parents would answer "no" to this question; therefore, soy infant formula has no place on the market today. Giving a baby soy formula can interrupt or disturb the normal hormonal cycle that is an important period of growth and development in a newborn. As an infant formula, soy should be avoided at all costs.

More on the issues with soy and soy formula can be found at http://www.soyonlineservice.co.nz.

[1] Lancet. 1997;3530(9070):23-27

[2] New Zealand Med. J. 5.24.1995, p. 318

[3] *Fort P, Moses N, Fasano M, Goldberg T, Lifshitz F.J Am Coll Nutr. 1990 Apr;9(2):164-7*

[4] Neurotoxicology. 23(2002):645-51

[5] *Pediatrics Vol. 121 No. 5 May 2008, pp. 1062-1068 (doi:10.1542/peds.2008-0564)*

[6] *Pediatrics.* Apr 1997;99(4):505-12

[7] Mothering. Issue 124. May/June 2004.

[8] Am.J.Dis. Child. 1986. Dec;140(12):1263-7

[9] Toxicol Ind Health. 1998 Jan-Apr;14(1-2):223-37.

7

Soy and Allergies

Introduction

Soy milk is often recommended as an alternative for those with dairy allergies. Unfortunately, soy allergies are very common. Many people don't realize their persistent allergy symptoms may be caused by eating soy because it is hidden in so many food items.

Our testing has shown that soy is one of the most allergenic foods. This chapter will give you more information about allergies to soy, the danger of soy for those with allergies, and information about the link between peanut allergies and soy consumption.

Frequently Asked Questions

What Is A Food Allergy?

Food allergies occur when the immune system produces an inflammatory response to a substance (e.g., dust, pollen, food, etc). Sometimes the response can occur immediately, or it can take days or weeks to manifest. Delayed responses are actually more common and make it harder to pinpoint the culprit. Symptoms such as ear infections, sinus issues, aches and pains, chronic fatigue, and digestive complaints fall into this category.

Are Soy Allergies Common?

Yes. Soy is one of the top eight allergens along with dairy, egg, wheat, peanuts, tree nuts, fish, and shellfish. These eight allergens cause about 90% of all food allergy reactions. Approximately 2% of adults and 8% of children have some sort of food allergy. For some, food allergens result in anaphylaxis or a severe immune response requiring emergency care.

What About Soy If You Have Peanut Allergies?

Soy seems to be underestimated as a cause of food anaphylaxis especially in young children and those with peanut allergies. Soy allergies also seem to go hand in hand with other legume allergies. Keep in mind, soy is in the legume family and peanuts are actually legumes. People who have severe peanut allergies have been shown to react to soy. According to a three year study done in Sweden, 61 reactions to food allergies occurred, with 45 of the 61 resulting from peanuts, soy, and tree nuts. There were four fatal reactions attributed to soy. The four who died from anaphylaxis to soy had no known allergy to soy but had a severe allergy to peanuts.[1]

If you have a peanut allergy, you may be at risk for a severe soy reaction and should avoid soy and all food that contains soy derivatives.

What About Soy And Other Food Allergies?

Soy is a common food source for those on a gluten- or dairy-free diet. In the case of celiac disease (intolerance to gluten), research shows intestinal healing may not occur if soy is consumed in the diet. A 1999 study in the Scandinavian Journal of Gastroenterology illustrated that some adults with celiac disease experienced diarrhea, headache, nausea, and flatulence even on a gluten-free diet whenever they ate a tiny amount of soy.[2]

What If I Do Not Have A Severe Allergic Response When I Eat Soy?

Even though you may not have an extreme allergic reaction, it is still possible you may have a mild to moderate reaction. In this case, the reaction can be less severe than anaphylaxis. The continual ingestion of a mild to moderate food allergen can lead to a myriad of symptoms that are often difficult to relate to a food allergy. Symptoms such as gas and bloating are examples of these types of reactions. These symptoms can be related to leaky gut that is caused by a food allergy. Sometimes it is necessary to go on an elimination diet in order to pinpoint exactly which foods seem to be causing the most trouble. Holistic measures to heal the gut should also be taken with the guidance of a qualified health care practitioner.

What Is A Leaky Gut?

Leaky gut syndrome occurs when the bowel becomes damaged. This damage literally causes "holes" in the gastrointestinal lining. When this occurs, items that should not have access to the blood stream now gain access. This can include food allergens. In a healthy gastrointestinal tract, there is a barrier that prevents toxic substances from being absorbed. If there is too much irritation in the gastrointestinal tract, the cells of the intestine start to pull apart or become leaky. This extra space between them may allow food particles that are normally not absorbed to gain access to the blood system. When this happens, the immune system is exposed to foreign substances in the blood stream and becomes overactive. The end result is the production of chemicals (antibodies) to bind to these foreign substances. If there is a chronic leaky gut situation occurring, it can result in a persistently overactive immune system which may eventually lead to autoimmune disorders.

A large part of the treatment for leaky gut is to provide the body with the proper nutrients in order to heal the gut lining and decrease inflammation. Furthermore, the identification of the offending foods can allow the patient to remove the problem foods from the diet.

What Can Happen When There Is A Leaky Gut?

In a leaky gut, the barrier from the gastrointestinal tract to the bloodstream is damaged. This can lead to viruses, bacteria, parasites, and other toxic items getting free access to the blood stream. Food is not sterile. Viruses, bacteria, and even parasites are normal constituents of many foods and also normal constituents living in our gut. However, when they over-proliferate or enter the blood stream, they wreak havoc with the immune and nervous systems. Patients with leaky gut can experience mood and behavior changes, headaches, depression, muscle aches, fatigue, inability to concentrate, and brain fog.

Furthermore, young patients affected by these substances can also exhibit many of the behaviors and symptoms common in autism. In fact, abnormal intestinal permeability (or "leaky gut") was found in 43% of autistic children showing no intestinal signs or symptoms.[3] Healing leaky gut is an important factor in reducing the symptoms of autism. In fact, healing of the gut is often necessary to begin to ensure a full recovery from autism.

How Can I Tell If I Have Food Allergies?

The only sure way to be certain you have a particular food allergy is to have a trial of avoiding the allergenic food source for a period of time (generally 6-9 weeks) and then slowly reintroduce the food one at a time to see if you have a noticeable reaction. However, if your health improves on an elimination diet, it may be best to continue to avoid that food. A knowledgeable health care practitioner can help guide you through a food allergy avoidance program.

Is Soy A Good Alternative If You Are Avoiding Gluten, Casein, Or Dairy?

No. Unfortunately many people on gluten-, casein-, and/or dairy-free diets often turn to soy as a good alternative.

Soy is not a good replacement and may cause further adverse effects as discussed in Chapter 2. It is extremely difficult to find gluten and casein-free items that do not contain soy especially if you are looking to purchase packaged and processed foods. The key is to use real, whole foods and prepare as many items in your own kitchen as you can. Please refer to our books **The Guide to a Gluten-Free Diet, 2nd Edition** and **The Guide to a Dairy-Free Diet**.

Are All Soy Products Allergenic?

The allergens in soybeans reside in the protein fraction of the bean. The allergenic potential of specific soy foods and/or ingredients is largely based on processing techniques and the amount of protein or protein residue remaining in the final product. The majority of soy lecithin used in food applications is derived from refined soybean oil that has been processed using the hot-solvent extraction technique, which eliminates most, if not all, allergenic proteins. Though this might be the case, some people with soy allergy are sensitive to soy lecithin as well.[4] We suggest you use caution with all forms of soy. If you have soy allergies, we suggest you refer to your doctor on whether or not to include soy lecithin in your diet.

Final Thought

Many people who try to avoid meat and dairy turn to soy. However, soy is not a healthy replacement and is actually very highly allergenic. Those suffering from allergies may notice significant improvement from their symptoms as soy is removed from the diet. We have found that a significant percentage of our patients are sensitive to soy—we estimate the number at well over 50%. Soy is not a healthy substitute for dairy. Any allergy elimination program should include soy in the removal phase.

[1] Allergy. 54(3):261-265. March 1999. Foucard, T; Yman, I. Malmheden

[2] *Scandinavian Journal of Gastroenterology*, Volume 34, Number 8, 24 August 1999, pp. 784-789(6)

[3] *Acta Paediatr. 1996 Sep;85(9):1076-9.*

[4] Bush, Taylor, Nordlee, Busse. Soybean oil is not allergenic to soybean-sensitive individuals. J Allergy Clin Immunol. 1985;76:242-245.

8

Soy and Genetically Modified Foods

Introduction

Soy is one of the most common genetically modified (GM) foods in the food supply today as approximately 90% of the soy on the market today is genetically modified. As of this writing, the FDA does not require any safety testing or any labeling of GM foods.

What is a GM food? Genetically modified foods have had their DNA altered. Scientists accomplish this by inserting certain genes into the DNA of the plant. For example, in the case of the majority of soy, researchers have inserted a gene that makes the soy plant resistant to the pesticide Roundup®. Therefore, in order to control weeds, soy plants can be sprayed liberally with Roundup® without hurting the soy plants. Scientists and advocates believe that altering the DNA of plants will increase the yield of crops and maximize profits. Furthermore, they claim this process is done for the good of all people as it will result in stronger plants and an increased yield which will help feed the world. Unfortunately, with the growth of GM foods becoming more common, we are all being experimented upon. Since the proper studies have not been completed, no one knows the long-term effects of these genetically modified foods.

Could the introduction of new genes into a fruit or vegetable create unknown results such as new toxins, bacteria, allergens, or diseases? What if there have been studies on animals showing pre-cancerous cell growth, damaged immune systems, and higher death rates after eating genetically modified foods? What if the government was not doing any safety testing on these potentially dangerous foods increasingly found in our food supply? We will answer these questions in this chapter as well as teach you about what GM foods are and how to avoid them. For more about GM foods and GMO's (genetically modified organisms) in our food supply, we refer you to the books *Seeds of Deception* and *Genetic Roulette*, by Jeffrey Smith or the website www.seedsofdeception.com.

Frequently Asked Questions

What Is A Genetically Modified Food?

A genetically modified (GM) food is a food derived from genetically modified organisms (GMO's). Through genetic engineering, scientists have discovered how to change the DNA blueprint of certain foods. They take the genetic material (DNA) from one species and transfer it into another in order to obtain a desired trait. Genetic engineering is done in order to improve the yield of the crops which, of course, helps to maximize profits. As previously mentioned, in the case of soy, scientists have inserted a gene in the soy DNA that makes it resistant to the pesticide Roundup®. Farmers can spray copious amounts of Roundup® on the GM soy crop (containing the Roundup® gene) in order to kill the weeds without harming the soy plant. What is the problem with this process? This process ensures that the final product available to consumers will contain residues of pesticides such as Roundup®. Furthermore, it is only a matter of time until the weeds become resistant to Roundup®. Then, farmers will have more problems on their hands trying to control "super-weeds" that are resistant to pesticides. Studies have shown that Roundup® can cause brain, intestinal, and heart defects in fetuses. Animal studies have shown that ingestion of GM modified soy results in infertility, an altered immune system, and a higher death rate.[1]

Are GM Foods Identical To Conventional Foods?

Genetically modified (GM) foods may look and feel the same as conventional foods, but they are drastically different.

GM foods are promoted to help make crops resistant to disease, to increase protein and vitamin levels making food more nutritious, and to make fruit and vegetables last longer. However, when the DNA of a crop is altered by adding the genes of bacteria, viruses, insects, animals, or even humans, the resulting effects cannot be predicted. Many studies show there are damaging side effects to this process and that it may not be in our best interest to consume these foods. Common sense would hold that this process should only be undertaken after careful study. Unfortunately, this has not been done.

What Are The Dangers Of Eating GMO's?

Many people are particularly sensitive to GM foods, especially soy. This is because GM foods introduce antigens or bacteria not originally found in the food source. There are issues with potential toxins, allergens, carcinogens, new diseases, antibiotic resistant diseases, and nutritional problems that may occur with ingesting GM foods and GMO's. Children are particularly at risk since they are still in the growth stages and are more susceptible to GMO effects.

How Much Soy Is Genetically Modified?

Genetically modified soybean varieties began to be commercially grown in 1996. Soy is one of the most common GM foods along with corn, cottonseed, and canola. As previously mentioned, approximately 90% of soy grown in the U.S. is genetically modified. Soybeans are genetically modified by inserting an herbicide resistant gene taken from bacteria into the soybean making the soybean resistant to herbicides (e.g., Roundup®). Interestingly, the big conglomerate Monsanto produces both the Roundup Ready® soy seeds and the herbicide Roundup®. GM soy may help the soy industry by increasing the yield and making the soy industry more profitable. However, common sense would dictate that GM soy surely cannot be beneficial to our digestive and immune systems due to the introduction of foreign genes into a food source. The gene introduced into the soy plant has never been part of the human food supply. Other items in our food supply that are affected by GM soy include ingredients derived from soy. The only soy that is not genetically modified is organic soy. If you eat soy, we recommend only organic, fermented soy.

Are Food Labels Accurate? Do They Tell You If A Food Source is Genetically Modified?

Unfortunately, there is no regulation on GM labeling and there also is no monitoring of the impacts GM food may be having on human health. However, because soy is one of the top eight food allergens, manufacturers are required to list it on labels due to The Food Allergen Labeling and Consumer Protection Act passed in 2006. This is helpful in avoiding GM soy because any food with soy in it has to list it. Furthermore, if the soy is not organic then it is more than likely GM soy. Also, soy is often hidden in colors, flavors, or spice blends added to foods and it should be listed on the label.

How Can You Avoid GMO's?

First of all, be aware of the most common GMO foods, which include soy, corn, canola, and cottonseed. Many processed foods contain these ingredients or their derivatives (e.g., corn syrup, high fructose corn syrup, soy lecithin, soy protein). Be careful of meat, eggs, and dairy from animals fed GM feed. Also, even many non-food items may have GMO's in them such as cosmetics, detergents, and bath products. Only certified organic foods are not allowed to have GMO ingredients or have been fed

GM feed. As for beauty items and cosmetics the regulations for organic on the labels are not as strict as for food and so you need to do your own research to find companies you trust. Many manufacturers will state on their label if their ingredients are "non-GMO". Finding local farmers and sources for organic and GMO-free foods is a great way to go. Additionally, visit www.responsibletechnology.org, where you can download a GMO-free shopping guide.

Keep in mind, the FDA does not regulate GMO's and relies on the Biotech industry for their information without requiring any safety studies. Since the FDA is busy protecting the big agribusinesses, it is up to you to find out what foods have GMO's and what foods you should or should not be eating. Be careful when eating out because many restaurants (especially fast food places) use GM foods. GM soy is in many fast food items. A great documentary confronting this issue is called *Hidden Dangers in Kids' Meals: Genetically Engineered Foods*.

Final Thoughts

Reading labels is important to avoid GMO's. Look for "non-GMO" or "Made without genetically modified ingredients" on the label and buy organic products whenever possible. Generally, if a food label states the product contains soy, you can assume it contains GM soy. Generally, non-GMO soy will be listed as such. We suggest that it is best to avoid all forms of non fermented soy. However, if soy is going to be eaten, it is best to eat organic, non-GMO soy. Be aware of where GM soy might be found such as soy lecithin in chocolate, soy flour in breads, soy protein in shakes and bars, and soy milk in baby formulas. More items containing soy are listed in Chapters 1 and 2. Of course, making things at home in your own kitchen with ingredients you trust is your safest bet to avoid soy and GM foods.

[1] The Independent Environment.co.uk 1.8.2006

9

Tips and Recipes

Introduction

Soy is hidden in numerous items. Soybean oil and soy flour are in many baked goods, sauces, dressings, and many common packaged foods. Beware of soy in common food items like canned tuna and soups, chocolate, frozen dinners, pizza, bread, muffins, and cake mixes. The best way to avoid soy is to prepare food items at home. Use these tips and recipes to guide you. Experimentation will be the key to finding what works best for you and your family.

Tips To Avoid Soy:

- Use real fats like butter, coconut oil, or olive oil. Avoid processed vegetable oils, butter substitutes, shortening, and spreads which often contain soybean oil.

- Make homemade salad dressings (see recipes Pages 146-149) and avoid store-bought dressings which often have soybean oil as the main ingredient.

- Prepare fresh foods at home and avoid canned goods, frozen meals, and vegetables which often contain soybean oil or soy flour.

- Use coconut milk or homemade almond milk (see recipe page 132) and avoid soy milk for drinking or cooking.

- Avoid protein bars or shakes that contain soy protein isolate.

- Be wary of breads, muffins, and baked goods that often have soy flour and also soybean oil (usually hydrogenated) in them.

- Look out for those hidden names that could be soy such as "textured vegetable protein" (TVP®), "textured plant protein", "hydrolyzed vegetable protein" (HVP), "vegetable oil", "MSG" (monosodium glutamate), "lecithin", "vegetable broth", "bouillon", and "natural flavorings."

- Read labels every time you make a purchase, especially if you have soy allergies. Manufacturers often change their ingredients and their labels. One day an item may not have soy and the next day it might!

- Check your vitamins, supplements, over-the-counter-drugs, prescriptions, and beauty products all of which may contain soy in some form.

- Cook and prepare your meals at home with fresh, whole foods to avoid soy that is hidden in over 60% of the items in grocery stores.

Recipes

These recipes are meant to give you a basic start for a healthy lifestyle. Many of the recipes are kid-friendly, too! Many people have used soy to replace meat and dairy. Hence, please note that all of the recipes in this book are meat-free and dairy-free, as well as gluten-free. For more recipes, please refer to our other books entitled ***The Guide to Healthy Eating, 2nd Edition, The Guide to a Gluten-Free Diet 2nd Edition***, and ***The Guide to a Dairy-Free Diet***. Although you can find many pre-made and packaged items at a variety of stores, we encourage you to prepare as many items as you can at home.

NOTE: When purchasing the ingredients to make the following recipes, the authors are assuming you are buying gluten-, dairy-, and soy-free versions of each listed ingredient.

Breakfast and Snack Recipes (Pages 132-136)

- ❖ Almond Milk
- ❖ Avocado Fruit Smoothie
- ❖ Blueberry Mini Muffins
- ❖ Chia Seed Smoothie
- ❖ Spice Muffins

Lunch and Dinner Recipes (Pages 137-145)

- ❖ Cinnamon Sweet Potato Puree
- ❖ Coconut Green Beans
- ❖ Ginger Quinoa Squash
- ❖ Lemon Tahini Kale
- ❖ Lentil Sweet Potato Soup
- ❖ Many Bean Chili
- ❖ Sloppy Lentils
- ❖ Tempeh Quinoa Stir-Fry
- ❖ Vegetable Rice Stir-Fry

Dressing Recipes (Pages 146-149)

- ❖ Balsamic Dressing
- ❖ Creamy Coconut Balsamic Dressing
- ❖ Honey Mustard Dressing
- ❖ Lemon Tahini Dressing

Dip Recipes (Pages 150-153)

- ❖ Guacamole Dip
- ❖ Hummus Dip
- ❖ Pineapple Chipotle Salsa Dip
- ❖ Salsa Dip

Dessert Recipes (Pages 154-160)

- ❖ Black Bean Brownies
- ❖ Cashew-Chocolate Frosting
- ❖ Coconut Cacao Bites
- ❖ Flourless Chocolate Cake
- ❖ Peach Coconut Milk Ice Cream
- ❖ Pumpkin Spice Cake
- ❖ Whipped Cashew Cream

BREAKFAST AND SNACK RECIPES

Almond Milk

½	cup raw almonds
1½	cups filtered water
1	teaspoon raw honey
½	teaspoon vanilla
2	dashes cinnamon
1	dash nutmeg

Servings: 4   Prep: 5 minutes

Cover almonds with filtered water and let soak overnight. Drain and keep the water. Put almonds in a blender (Vita-Mix recommended) and blend until butter-like. You may need to add a small amount of the water to help them blend well. Add back the water you drained from almonds and the rest of the ingredients. Blend completely. Add ice if desired and blend until smooth. Refrigerate.

Avocado Fruit Smoothie

½	avocado, ripe
1	cups mangoes, frozen
½	cup strawberries, frozen
½	cup filtered water
½	cup almond milk, see recipe (Page 132) or use water
1-2	teaspoons raw honey (or to taste)

Servings: 1-2

Prep: 5 minutes   Blend: 2 minutes

Add all ingredients to blender. Blend until smooth and serve.

Blueberry Mini Muffins

3	free-range, organic eggs
3	tablespoons raw honey
3	tablespoons ghee (or ghee/coconut oil blend)
1	teaspoon vanilla paste (or extract)
5	drops stevia or vanilla stevia
¾	cup coconut flour, sifted
1	teaspoon baking soda
½	cup blueberries

Servings: 20 mini muffins

Prep: 10 minutes   Cook: 14-16 minutes

Whisk eggs. Blend in honey, ghee, vanilla, and stevia. Add coconut flour and baking soda and mix until smooth. Stir in blueberries. Scoop 2 teaspoons batter into greased mini muffin pan and bake 14-16 minutes at 325°F.

Chia Seed Smoothie

1	cup coconut milk
1	cup strawberries, frozen
1	banana, fresh or frozen
1	tablespoon chia seeds

Servings: 1-2

Prep: 5 minutes   Blend: 2 minutes

Mix together in a blender until smooth and creamy. Add filtered water if necessary to desired consistency.

Spice Muffins

2	cups brown rice flour
2	teaspoon baking soda
1 ½	teaspoons sea salt
1 ½	teaspoons cinnamon
½	teaspoon xanthan gum
⅛	teaspoon ginger
⅛	teaspoon clove
⅓	cup coconut oil
⅓	cup Sucanat™, raw cane sugar
⅓	cup raw honey
1 ½	cup applesauce
½	cup raisins
½	cup walnuts (optional)

Servings: 20-22

Prep: 10 minutes   Cook: 20 minutes

Preheat oven to 350°F. Mix first seven dry ingredients together in bowl. In another bowl beat oil and sweeteners, then add applesauce. Slowly mix dry ingredients into oil mixture. Stir in raisins and walnuts by hand if using. Put into muffin pan and bake approximately 20 minutes.

LUNCH AND DINNER RECIPES

Cinnamon Sweet Potato Puree

2	large sweet potatoes
⅔	cup coconut milk
2	teaspoons cinnamon
2	tablespoons vanilla paste or extract
2-3	teaspoons maple syrup (or to taste)
½	teaspoon sea salt

Servings: 4

Prep: 10 minutes   Cook: 60 minutes

Preheat oven to 400°F. Cut sweet potatoes in half and bake in center of oven for 1 hour or until tender when pierced with a fork. While baking warm the coconut milk and cinnamon in a small sauce pan. Remove potatoes from oven and scoop flesh into a food processor. Process potatoes until they are smooth. Add vanilla, maple syrup, and sea salt and then process again. Put into a bowl and fold in the coconut milk and cinnamon mixture. Serve warm.

Coconut Green Beans

1	tablespoon coconut oil
½	cup onion, chopped
2	tablespoons water
2	cloves garlic, minced
1	pound green beans, ends removed
1½	cups tomato, diced
¾	cup coconut milk
½	teaspoon sea salt

Servings: 4-6

Prep: 10 minutes   Cook: 20 minutes

Sauté onion in coconut oil over medium-high heat for about 3-5 minutes. Add water, garlic, and green beans. Stir fry for 8-10 minutes until desired texture. Add tomatoes, coconut milk, and sea salt and heat through.

Ginger Quinoa Squash

1	butternut squash
½	cup quinoa
¾	cup water
½	teaspoon ginger
1-2	tablespoons organic butter
1	teaspoon raw honey

Servings: 4

Prep: 10 minutes   Cook: 85 minutes

Preheat oven to 300°F. Cut butternut squash in half and remove seeds. Place skin side up into about 1 inch of water in a Pyrex dish and bake at 300°F for about 55 minutes or until tender. While squash is baking, make quinoa by rinsing it and placing it in a saucepan covered with ¾ cup water. Bring water to boil, turn down heat and simmer about 20 minutes or until tender; set aside. Remove cooked squash from skin and mash in a small pan. Stir in ginger and butter and heat over low heat. Add cooked quinoa and top with honey before serving.

Note: *For optimal results with Quinoa (and for optimal digestion), we suggest you soak your quinoa overnight as follows– 1 cup quinoa, 2 cups filtered water, and 2 tablespoons lemon juice. Rinse quinoa after soaking. Add to cooking water and cook as recipe describes.*

Serving Suggestions: *Serve in the skin from the squash.*

Lemon Tahini Kale

1½	tablespoons tahini
1	tablespoon cold pressed flax oil
1	tablespoon extra virgin olive oil
1	lemon, juiced
2	teaspoons Ume plum vinegar
½	teaspoon naturally fermented soy sauce (shoyu)
1	head kale

Servings: 4

Prep: 10 minutes   Cook: 10 minutes

Combine all ingredients except the kale in a food processor and mix until smooth. Steam kale and chop or tear into pieces. Pour lemon tahini sauce over kale and serve.

Serving Suggestion: Lemon tahini sauce also makes a great salad dressing – see page 149!

Lentil Sweet Potato Soup

1	onion, chopped
2	tablespoons coconut oil
5	cups water
⅛	teaspoon cumin
⅛	teaspoon coriander
½	teaspoon turmeric
2	bay leaves
2	teaspoons sea salt
1	cup red lentils (uncooked)
1	large sweet potato, chopped
4-5	carrots, chopped

Servings: 4

Prep: 20 minutes   Cook: 50 minutes

In a large pot, sauté onion in coconut oil until tender. Stir in water and spices. Add lentils, sweet potato, and carrots and bring to boil. Skim froth at top if necessary, reduce heat, and simmer covered for about 45 minutes.

Many Bean Chili

1	cup kidney beans (canned or cooked)
1	cup great northern beans (canned or cooked)
1	cup pinto beans (canned or cooked)
1	cup black beans (canned or cooked)
3	cups diced tomatoes
⅓	cup tomato paste
½	cup filtered water
½	onion, diced
½	green pepper, diced
2	teaspoons chili powder
3	teaspoons cumin

Sea salt, pepper, cayenne to taste

Servings: 4

Prep: 15 minutes   Cook: 3-4 hours (crock pot)

Drain and rinse beans before placing them into a crock pot. Add the rest of the ingredients and stir completely. Cover and cook in crock pot for 3-4 hours.

Note: *For optimal results with non-canned beans (and for optimal digestion), we suggest you soak your beans overnight as follows before cooking– 1 cup beans, 2 cups filtered water, and 2 tablespoons lemon juice. Rinse beans after soaking.*

Sloppy Lentils

1½	cups lentils (uncooked)
3	cups filtered water
1	tablespoon lemon juice
½	cup onion, chopped
3	cups tomatoes, diced
1	tablespoon chili powder
2	teaspoons cumin
1	teaspoon sea salt
2	tablespoons Worcestershire sauce
1	tablespoon Dijon mustard
1	tablespoon maple syrup

Servings: 6

Prep: 20 minutes   Cook: 4-6 hours (crock pot)

Soak lentils overnight in water with lemon juice. Drain and rinse before placing into a crock pot. Add the rest of the ingredients to the crock pot with the lentils. Cover and cook on low-heat setting 4-6 hours. Lentils should be soft enough to eat. Serve over toast or with quinoa.

Tempeh Quinoa Stir-Fry

8	ounces tempeh, chopped into bite-size chunks
3	tablespoons coconut oil
½	cup yellow pepper, chopped into bite-size pieces
½	cup red pepper, chopped into bite-size pieces
½	cup red onion, chopped bite into bite-size pieces
2	cups portabella mushrooms, chopped into bite-size pieces
2	cloves garlic, minced
3	tablespoons naturally fermented soy sauce (shoyu)
1	tablespoon brown rice vinegar
2	teaspoons toasted sesame oil
1	teaspoon raw honey
⅔	cup quinoa, cooked

Servings: 4

Prep: 15 minutes   Cook: 25-28 minutes

Steam tempeh for 15 minutes and set aside. In deep sauté pan, heat coconut oil over medium heat. Add onions and peppers and sauté 3-5 minutes. While sautéing, whisk together sauce: garlic, soy sauce, vinegar, sesame oil, and honey and set aside. Add mushrooms and tempeh to peppers and onions along with sauce. Simmer 5-8 minutes stirring frequently. Stir in quinoa and serve.

Note: *For optimal results with Quinoa (and for optimal digestion), we suggest you soak your quinoa overnight as follows– 1 cup quinoa, 2 cups filtered water, and 2 tablespoons lemon juice. Rinse quinoa after soaking. Add to cooking water and cook as recipe describes.*

Vegetable Rice Stir-Fry

¼	cup onion, chopped
½	teaspoon ground ginger
½	teaspoon garlic or 1 clove, chopped
3	tablespoons coconut oil
3	tablespoons water
2	carrots, chopped
1	red pepper, chopped
½	zucchini, chopped
½	head kale, chopped
3	tablespoons fermented soy sauce (shoyu)
½	cup raw slivered almonds
1	cup brown or wild rice, cooked

Servings: 2-3

Prep: 25 minutes   Cook: 15 minutes

Sauté the onions, ginger, and garlic in coconut oil over medium-high heat for 4-5 minutes or until tender. Add water and the rest of the vegetables and stir-fry in the pan. When vegetables are close to being done, add soy sauce and almonds. Stir cooked rice into vegetables and serve.

DRESSING RECIPES

Balsamic Dressing

2	tablespoons aged Balsamic vinegar
1	teaspoon Dijon mustard
½	teaspoon sea salt
1	clove garlic, minced
¼	cup extra virgin olive oil
1	teaspoon cold-pressed flax oil

Servings: 4   Prep: 10 minutes

Combine balsamic, mustard, salt, and garlic in food processor. While processing, add olive oil in slow stream and then flax oil. Refrigerate before serving.

Creamy Coconut Balsamic Dressing

⅛	cup coconut milk
1½	tablespoons aged Balsamic vinegar
1	teaspoon Dijon mustard
½	teaspoon dried basil
¼	teaspoon sea salt
¼	cup extra virgin olive oil
2	teaspoons cold-pressed flax oil

Servings: 4   Prep: 10 minutes

Combine coconut milk, balsamic, mustard, basil, and salt in food processor. While processing, add olive oil in slow stream and then flax oil. Refrigerate before serving.

Honey Mustard Dressing

¼	cup lemon juice
2	tablespoons Dijon mustard
2	tablespoons raw honey
1	clove garlic, minced
1	dash cayenne pepper
½	cup extra virgin olive oil
2	teaspoons cold-pressed flax oil

Servings: 4   Prep: 10 minutes

Combine lemon juice, mustard, honey, garlic, and cayenne pepper in food processor. While processing, add olive oil in slow stream and then flax oil. Refrigerate before serving.

Lemon Tahini Dressing

1½	tablespoons tahini
1	tablespoon cold-pressed flax oil
1	tablespoon extra virgin olive oil
1	lemon, juiced
2	teaspoons Ume plum vinegar
½	teaspoon naturally fermented soy sauce (shoyu)

Servings: 4   Prep: 10 minutes

Combine all ingredients in a food processor and mix until smooth. Refrigerate.

DIP RECIPES

Guacamole Dip

2	avocados, ripe
2	tablespoons lemon
1	cup tomato, chopped
¼	cup onion, chopped
2	cloves garlic, minced
2	teaspoons sea salt
¼	teaspoon cayenne

Servings: 4-6   Prep: 10-15 minutes

First scoop avocados out of their shells and mash them in a bowl. Cover with lemon juice to prevent browning. Add remaining ingredients and mix well. Chill and serve.

Serving Suggestions: *Great with blue chips or on salads.*

Hummus Dip

2	cups garbanzo beans (canned or cooked)
2	cloves garlic, crushed
3	tablespoons tahini
½	cup lemon juice
1	teaspoon cumin
2	dashes cayenne (add to taste)
¼	teaspoon sea salt

Servings: 6   Prep: 15 minutes

Process cooked garbanzo beans in food processor until smooth. Add remaining ingredients and blend to desired consistency.

Note: To make smoother, add 2 tablespoons water and 1 tablespoon olive oil.

Serving Suggestion: *Put in bowl and pour 1 tablespoon olive oil over top, sprinkle with paprika, kalamata olives, and parsley.*

Note: *For optimal results with non-canned beans (and for optimal digestion), we suggest you soak your beans overnight as follows before cooking– 1 cup beans, 2 cups filtered water, and 2 tablespoons lemon juice. Rinse beans after soaking.*

Pineapple Chipotle Salsa Dip

2	tablespoons coconut oil
3	cups pineapple, diced
1½	cups onion, chopped
1	cup seeded tomato, diced
2	cloves garlic, minced
½	cup pineapple juice
2	tablespoons Sucanat™
2	tablespoons apple cider vinegar
1	chipotle chili in adobo sauce, drained and minced
1	tablespoon adobo sauce (from drained chilies)
½	cup parsley, finely chopped
2	tablespoons fresh lime juice
½	teaspoon sea salt

Servings: 8

Prep: 10-15 minutes   Cook: 15-17 minutes

Heat the coconut oil in a large skillet over medium-high heat. Add pineapple and onion, sauté 5-7 minutes or until lightly browned. Add tomato and garlic, sauté 2 minutes. Stir in pineapple juice, Sucanat™, vinegar, chilies, and adobo sauce. Cook 6-8 minutes stirring occasionally. Remove from heat and stir in parsley, lime juice, and sea salt. Chill and serve.

Salsa Dip

1	small Vidalia onion
½	cup cilantro
3	cloves garlic
3	cups tomatoes, diced
2-4	dashes cayenne (add to desired hotness)
2	tablespoons lime (or lemon)
¼	teaspoon sea salt

Servings: 8   Prep: 10-15 minutes

In food processor chop onion, cilantro, and garlic. Then add tomatoes and the rest of the ingredients and process until smooth.

Serving Suggestions: Chop and mix salsa by hand for a chunkier salsa. *Use jalapeños and seeds if you want a hotter salsa.*

DESSERT RECIPES

Black Bean Brownies

1½	cups black beans, cooked or canned
3	free-range, organic eggs
½	cup Sucanat™, raw cane sugar
¼	cup raw honey
2	teaspoons vanilla paste or extract
⅛	teaspoon sea salt
1½	cups chocolate chips
⅓	cup coconut oil

Servings: 8-12

Prep: 10 minutes   Cook: 25-30 minutes

Preheat oven to 350°F. Drain and rinse black beans. In food processor combine black beans, eggs, Sucanat™, honey, vanilla, and sea salt. In small saucepan, melt chocolate chips and coconut oil. Add chocolate mixture to food processor and process until smooth. Pour into greased 8X8 Pyrex® dish (try using coconut oil). Bake 25-30 minutes or until set. Cool before cutting and serving.

Note: *For optimal results with non-canned beans (and for optimal digestion), we suggest you soak your beans overnight as follows before cooking– 1 cup beans, 2 cups filtered water, and 2 tablespoons lemon juice. Rinse beans after soaking.*

Cashew-Chocolate Frosting

½	cup cashew butter
½	cup chocolate chips
¼	cup raw honey

Frosts: 1-8X8 cake

Prep: 5 minutes   Cook: 5 minutes

In small sauce pan, combine cashew butter, chocolate chips, and honey. Stir over medium-low heat until melted. Let cool for 5 minutes before spreading on cake (has a fudge-like consistency when completely cooled).

Coconut Cacao Bites

⅓	cup raw honey
2	tablespoons coconut oil
3	tablespoons cacao powder
½	teaspoon cinnamon
¼	cup almond butter
½	cup rolled oats or crispy rice cereal
¼	cup coconut flour
1	teaspoon vanilla paste (or extract)

Servings: 1 dozen

Prep: 5 minutes   Cook: 5 minutes

In a saucepan over medium heat combine honey, coconut oil, cacao powder, and cinnamon. Stir continuously until chocolate syrup-like texture. Remove from heat and add remaining ingredients. Stir until completely combined. Drop by the spoonful on waxed paper and chill approximately 45 minutes or until firm and chewy.

Flourless Chocolate Cake

1 ½	cups garbanzo beans (canned or cooked)
1	cup chocolate chips
¼	cup cashew butter
3	free-range, organic eggs
¾	cup Sucanat™, whole cane sugar
1	teaspoon baking powder
¼	teaspoon sea salt
½	teaspoon vanilla

Servings: 6-8

Prep: 15 minutes   Cook: 30 minutes

Preheat oven to 350°F. Drain and rinse garbanzo beans and add to food processor. In small sauce pan, melt chocolate chips and cashew butter over low heat. Add to food processor along with remaining ingredients and process until smooth. Pour into a greased 8 X 8 inch Pyrex dish. Bake for about 30 minutes (use a toothpick to determine that it is cooked). Cool cake and frost, if desired.

Note: *For optimal results with non-canned beans (and for optimal digestion), we suggest you soak your beans overnight as follows before cooking– 1 cup beans, 2 cups filtered water, and 2 tablespoons lemon juice. Rinse beans after soaking.*

Serving Suggestion: Frost with Cashew-Chocolate Frosting (page 155).

Peach Coconut Milk Ice Cream

2	cups coconut milk
2	cups peaches, frozen
½	cup maple syrup
2	teaspoons vanilla paste (or extract)
1	pinch sea salt

Servings: 2   Prep: 5 minutes

Put all ingredients in blender and blend until smooth. Pour in ice cream machine and freeze according to the machine's instructions and serve.

Pumpkin Spice Cake

1	cup brown rice flour
1	teaspoon baking soda
½	teaspoon baking powder
½	teaspoon cinnamon
¼	teaspoon cloves
¼	teaspoon nutmeg
½	cup coconut oil
½	cup Sucanat™, whole cane sugar
2	free-range, organic eggs
1	cup pumpkin
½	cup chocolate chips (optional)

Servings: 6-8

Prep: 15 minutes   Cook: 35 minutes

Preheat oven to 300°F. In a small bowl, mix brown rice flour, baking soda, baking powder, cinnamon, cloves, and nutmeg; set aside. In a large mixing bowl, mix coconut oil and Sucanat™ together until creamy and then add eggs and pumpkin. Slowly pour the flour mixture into the pumpkin mixture and mix completely. Stir the chocolate chips (optional) in by hand. Bake in a well greased 8 X 8 inch Pyrex dish (try using coconut oil) for approximately 35 minutes.

Whipped Cashew Cream

1	cup raw cashews
1¼	cups warm, filtered water
½	teaspoon sea salt
1	teaspoon vanilla paste (or extract)
1	teaspoon raw honey or maple syrup

Servings: 2

Prep: 10 minutes   Soak time: 6 hours

Combine cashews, 1 cup filtered water, and sea salt. Let soak for 6 hours. Drain cashews and put in blender. Add the rest of the filtered water and the remaining ingredients and blend until smooth and creamy. Add more water if necessary. Chill before serving. Enjoy with fruit, pies, crisps, or other desserts!

APPENDIX A
Soy Descriptions

FERMENTED SOY

We suggest that you use these types of soy only in moderation.

Miso – produced by cooking soybeans along with a grain (e.g., barley, brown rice) and then fermenting the beans with salt and a culture in wooden tubs (i.e., cedar vats) for one to three years.

- Miso is a rich, salty, smooth paste used as a condiment in Japanese cooking. The Japanese make miso soup and use it to flavor a variety of foods. It is used to flavor soups, sauces, dressings, stir-fries, marinades, spreads, and pâtés.

- There are hundreds of types of miso. The darker kinds are saltier and more pungent, the lighter are sweeter and milder. Generally, only small amounts are used. Miso should be kept refrigerated. Miso contains many beneficial bacteria and enzymes and is useful for improving digestion and intestinal tract health. Always add miso to soups and stews at the end, since boiling it destroys beneficial bacteria and causes it to curdle.

Natto – produced by fermenting boiled whole soybeans with Bacillus natto culture.

- Natto has a strong taste and it has a sticky, viscous coating with a cheesy texture. In Asian countries, natto traditionally is served as a topping for rice, in soups, or in vegetable dishes.
- The fermentation process breaks down the beans' complex proteins making it easier to digest than whole soybeans. Natto is a valuable source of protein and has a high concentration of vitamin K. It is also loaded with nattokinase, a powerful blood-thinning enzyme.

Tempeh – produced by removing the hull of cooked, whole soybeans (sometimes mixed with another grain such as rice or millet) and then fermented with a culture and aged for one to two days.

- Tempeh is a good source of protein, fiber, and vitamins.
- Tempeh is a chunky, tender, rich cake of soybeans used traditionally in Indonesia. It has a chewy texture with a

smoky or nutty, mushroom-like flavor. Before being used, it needs to be steamed or simmered about 20 minutes. It can then be marinated, grilled, or fried, as well as added to soups, casseroles, sandwiches, stir-fries, or chili.

Fermented Soy Sauce – produced traditionally by fermenting soybeans, salt, and enzymes. Common types are Shoyu and Tamari.

- Used as a condiment – a salty, earthy, brownish liquid intended to season food while cooking or at the table.

- Be wary because many varieties of soy sauce on the market are made artificially using a chemical process and with hydrolyzed vegetable proteins (HVP).

NON-FERMENTED SOY

We suggest that you avoid this type of soy in your diet.

Edamamé (Green Vegetable Soybeans) – harvested when the beans are still green and sweet tasting. It is found shelled or still in the pod. It contains fewer of the toxins found in the mature beans.

Hydrolyzed Soy Protein – produced when the protein is broken down into amino acids by a chemical process known as acid hydrolysis. This is an extraction process where sulfuric acid is boiled and then neutralized with a caustic soda. The sludge is scraped off the top and dried. It contains MSG and other possibly harmful chemicals, many of which are cancer-causing. Hydrolyzed soy protein is used as a taste enhancer in many foods because it contains significant amounts of MSG. Oftentimes, these foods are not labeled as containing MSG. However, with any product containing hydrolyzed soy protein, you must assume that it is does contain MSG.

>More on MSG and its harmful side effects can be found in the book *Excitotoxins: The Taste That Kills*, by Russell Blaylock, M.D.

Lecithin – used in food manufacturing as an emulsifier in products high in fats and oils. It is extracted from soybean oil; it also functions as an antioxidant and promotes stabilization, crystallization, and spattering control of oils. Powdered lecithin can be found in natural and health food stores.

Meat Alternatives (Meat Analogs) – made from soybeans and contain soy protein or tofu and other ingredients mixed together to simulate various kinds of meat. These meat alternatives are sold as frozen, canned, or dried foods. These products can be used the same way as the foods they replace.

Nondairy Soy Frozen Dessert – Nondairy frozen desserts are made from soy milk or soy yogurt.

Soybean Oil – produced by extraction from whole soybeans. It is the most widely used oil in the U.S., accounting for more than 75 percent of our total vegetable fat and oil intake. Oil sold in the grocery store under the generic name "vegetable oil" is usually 100 percent soy oil or a blend of soy oil and other oils. Read the label to make certain you are not buying soybean oil.

Soy Cheese – a cheese substitute produced from soymilk. Some soy cheeses have soy protein isolate added as well as a vegetable oil such as canola or soybean oil. Its creamy texture makes it a substitute for sour cream or cream cheese and it can be found in a variety of flavors in natural food stores. Sometimes coloring is added to soy cheese, as well as texture boosters, like guar gums or carrageenan. Also, calcium and/or vitamins A and E are often added to it.

Soy Fiber (Okara, Soy Bran, Soy Isolate Fiber) – Soy fiber is often used as an additive for breads, cereals, and snacks. These are the three basic types of soy fiber:

1. Okara is a pulp fiber by-product of soymilk.
2. Soy bran is made from hulls (the outer covering of the soybean), which are removed during initial processing. The hulls contain a fibrous material which can be extracted and then refined for use as a food ingredient.
3. Soy isolate fiber, also known as structured protein fiber (SPF), is soy protein isolate in a fibrous form.

Soy Flour – produced by roasting soybeans and grinding them into a fine powder. There are three kinds of soy flour available:

- Natural or full-fat, which contains the natural oils found in the soybean.
- Defatted, which has the oils removed during processing.
- Lecithinated, which has had lecithin added to it.

Soy Grits – produced similar to soy flour, but rather than a fine powder, they are toasted and then they are cracked into coarse pieces.

Soy Infant Formula – Soy protein isolate powder is often used as a base for this type of formula (instead of cow's milk). Carbohydrates and fats are added to achieve a fluid similar to breast milk.

Soy Milk – produced by soaking, cooking, and blending the soybeans and then straining off the soy milk. It is often found in aseptic containers which are non-refrigerated and shelf stable. It can also be found in quart and half gallon containers in the dairy case at your grocery store. Soy milk can also be found as powder, which must be mixed with water. Soy milk often has added vitamin D, usually in the form of D2.

Soy Nut – made from whole soybeans soaked in water, drained, and then baked or roasted. Soy nuts are similar in texture and flavor to peanuts.

Soy Nut Butter – produced from roasted, whole soy nuts, which are then crushed and blended with soy oil and other ingredients. Soy nut butter has a slightly nutty taste.

Soy Protein Concentrate – produced from defatted soy flakes. It contains about 70 percent protein but retains some of the bean's dietary fiber. It is usually produced from genetically-modified soy.

Soy Protein Isolate (Isolated Soy Protein) – produced when the soy protein is removed from defatted soybean flakes. This is the most highly refined soy protein and often contains genetically-modified soy. Soy protein isolate possesses the greatest amount of protein (about 92%) of all soy products and is often found in protein powders and protein bars.

Soy Sprouts – produced by sprouting in the same way as other beans and seeds.

Soy Yogurt – produced from soy milk. Because it has a creamy texture, it is proclaimed to be an easy substitute for sour cream or cream cheese.

Textured Soy Flour – contains about 70 percent protein and retains most of the bean's dietary fiber. Often referred to simply as textured soy protein (TSP), textured soy flour is sold dried in granular and chunk style. It can be found in natural food stores and through mail-order catalogs.

Textured Soy Protein (TSP) – produced by running defatted soy flour through an extrusion cooker at high temperature and pressure. This allows for many different forms and sizes (chunks, flakes, nuggets, grains, and strips) of TSP. When hydrated it has a chewy texture. It is widely used as a meat extender.

- TSP usually refers to products made from textured soy flour, although the term can also be applied to textured soy protein concentrates and spun soy fiber.
- TSP is commonly found as a popular brand made by Archer Daniels Midland Company, which owns the right to the product named Textured Vegetable Protein (TVP®).

Tofu – produced by curdling fresh hot soy milk with a coagulant to make it soft and cheese-like. It is also known as soybean curd. Firm tofu is very dense and solid and is often cut up in cubes for soups, stir-frying, or grilling. Soft tofu is used when blended tofu is needed. Silken tofu is used as a sour cream replacement in dips and also in dressings.

Whole Soybeans – As soybeans mature in the pod, they ripen into a hard, dry bean. Most soybeans are yellow. However, there are brown and black varieties. Whole soybeans can be cooked and used in sauces, stews, and soups. When grown without agricultural chemicals, they are referred to as organically grown soybeans.

Appendix B
Soy-Free Start-Up Shopping Guide

NOTE: You can print a handy PDF version of this guide at www.aplacetobe.com, under the Resources link.

Always Read Labels

Do *not* purchase foods that contain any form of soy flour, isolate, concentrate, lecithin, or protein. Be wary of baby formulas, baked goods, crackers, marinades and sauces, mayonnaise, soups, dressings, veggie burgers, meat substitutes, dairy substitutes, ice cream, protein powders, and protein bars that may have soy.

Look At Allergen List On Labels

Since soy is one of the top eight allergens, manufacturers are now required to state on the label if there are any soy ingredients, just as they must identify the other major food allergens - milk, eggs, fish, crustacean shellfish, tree nuts, peanuts, and wheat.

Limit Processed And Packaged Foods

By limiting processed and packaged foods, you help to ensure you are not ingesting soy. Soy flour, soybean oil, soy protein, and soy lecithin are common ingredients in many foods. Making foods at home from fresh ingredients or eating at restaurants you trust is highly recommended.

Avoid Soy Infant Formula

Soy infant formula is not a good choice for babies even if they cannot be breastfed or cannot tolerate cow's milk formulas. For more information on alternatives, please refer to the children's health section at www.westonaprice.org.

Foods You *Can* Eat

Foods that you can eat include any items that do not contain soy or any soy derivative. Also, fermented forms of soy including miso, natto, and tempeh can be included in moderation. It is important to know whether the places you are going will have foods that you can eat.

Avoid Protein Bars And Powders

Most protein bars and powders use non-fermented soy as the source of protein. Be sure to double check labels and call manufacturers to be certain there is no soy protein isolate or concentrate in the product.

Try Coconut Milk

If you are avoiding dairy, instead of using soy milk, a healthy alternative is coconut milk. Rich in medium-chain-fatty acids and lauric acid, coconut milk is a wonderful health food. It's great in smoothies, for homemade ice cream, to make cream sauces, or in oatmeal!

Appendix C

Soy-Free Restaurant Guide

NOTE: You can print a handy PDF version of this guide at www.aplacetobe.com, under the Resources link.

Research And Always Call Ahead

Call ahead to find out if your restaurant choice can cater to your dietary needs. Avoid most fast food restaurants. Many higher-end restaurants will guide you through the menu and discuss the ingredients of each item so you can determine what items are soy-free ahead of time.

Explain Your Dietary Restrictions

It helps to find knowledgeable waiters or waitresses that will work with you and guide you through the menu. You can also explain that you are avoiding soy and ask if they or the chef can help you in ordering and preparing your meal soy-free.

Speak To The Chef

Speak with the chef about options that can be made soy-free and to ensure your food will not be cooked in soybean oil. Be sure to ask specifically what oil they use in cooking. Keep in mind "vegetable oil" is almost always soy, cottonseed, corn, or canola oil. Better choices for cooking include butter and coconut oil.

Items You Can Order

Stick to simple items such as grilled meat, fish, or poultry and a side of steamed vegetables, which are items least likely to have soy in them since there aren't sauces or breading. Ask what kind of oil the restaurant uses to cook with and if the meats, fish, or poultry may have been marinated in a soybean oil or dressing. Unless they make homemade salad dressings with olive oil, then opt for salads with simply lemon juice, olive oil, and vinegar. Always ask for dressings, spreads, and condiments on the side.

Items To Avoid

Avoid breaded foods, veggie burgers, meat or dairy substitutes, imitation foods, foods with sauces, dressings, or marinades that are not homemade and any other items for which the server or chef cannot tell you all the ingredients. Also, avoid any foods cooked in soybean oil.

Confirm Your Order And Be Grateful!

Prior to eating, be sure to double-check with your server that your meal was prepared without any soy or in any soybean oil. If you have a successful dining experience, gratitude can go a long way!

About the Authors

David Brownstein, M.D.

David Brownstein, M.D. is a family physician who utilizes the best of conventional and alternative therapies. He is the Medical Director for the Center for Holistic Medicine in West Bloomfield, MI. He is a graduate of the University of Michigan and Wayne State University School of Medicine. Dr. Brownstein is board certified by the American Academy of Family Physicians. He is a member of the American Academy of Family Physicians and the American College for the Advancement in Medicine. He is the father of two beautiful girls, Hailey and Jessica, and is a retired soccer coach.

Dr. Brownstein has lectured internationally about his success with using natural items. Dr. Brownstein has authored *Salt Your Way to Health, 2nd Edition*; *Iodine, Why You Need It, Why You Can't Live Without It, 4th Edition*; *The Miracle of Natural Hormones 3rd Edition*; *Overcoming Thyroid Disorders, 2nd Edition*; *Overcoming Arthritis*; *Drugs That Don't Work and Natural Therapies That Do, 2nd Edition*; *The Guide to Healthy Eating, 2nd Edition*; *The Guide to a Gluten-Free Diet, 2nd Edition*; and *The Guide to a Dairy-Free Diet*.

Dr. Brownstein is the author of **Dr. Brownstein's Natural Way to Health** Monthly Newsletter. His weekly blog can be accessed on his website at www.drbrownstein.com.

Dr. Brownstein's office is located at:
Center for Holistic Medicine
5821 W. Maple Rd., Ste. 192
West Bloomfield, MI 48323

P: 248.851.1600

www.centerforholisticmedicine.com
www.drbrownstein.com

Sheryl Shenefelt, C.N., CMTA

Sheryl Shenefelt is a Certified Nutritionist, Certified Metabolic Typing® Advisor, and co-author of **The Guide to Healthy Eating, 2nd Edition; The Guide to a Gluten-Free Diet, 2nd Edition** and **The Guide to a Dairy-Free Diet** with Dr. Brownstein. She lives with her wonderful husband Bob, and beautiful children, Grace and Nicholas. Sheryl's interest in health and nutrition peaked even further when she became pregnant with her first child, now nine-years-old, and with the desire to raise a healthy family. She has a passion for learning and researching about food and nutrition, as well as teaching those desiring to implement a more natural and organic lifestyle. She also does "Shop with Sheryl" classes to teach people how to shop for healthy foods.

For more about Sheryl, her recommended organic, natural, and gluten-free resources, please visit her website at www.aplacetobe.com.

Books by David Brownstein, M.D.
More information: www.drbrownstein.com

IODINE: WHY YOU NEED IT, WHY YOU CAN'T LIVE WITHOUT IT, 4th EDITION

Iodine is the most misunderstood nutrient. Dr. Brownstein shows you the benefit of supplementing with iodine. Iodine deficiency is rampant. Iodine deficiency is a world-wide problem and is at near epidemic levels in the United States. Most people wrongly assume that you get enough iodine from iodized salt. Dr. Brownstein convincingly shows you why it is vitally important to get your iodine levels measured. He shows you how iodine deficiency is related to:
- **Breast cancer**
- **Hypothyroidism and Graves' disease**
- **Autoimmune illnesses**
- **Chronic Fatigue and Fibromyalgia**
- **Cancer of the prostate, ovaries and much more!**

DRUGS THAT DON'T WORK and NATURAL THERAPIES THAT DO, 2nd Edition

Dr. Brownstein's newest book will show you why the most commonly prescribed drugs may not be your best choice. Dr. Brownstein shows why drugs have so many adverse effects. The following conditions are covered in this book: high cholesterol levels, depression, GERD and reflux esophagitis, osteoporosis, inflammation and hormone imbalances. He also gives examples of natural substances that can help the body heal. See why the following drugs need to be avoided:

- **Cholesterol-lowering drugs (statins such as Lipitor, Zocor, Mevacor, and Crestor and Zetia)**
- **Antidepressant drugs (SSRI's such as Prozac, Zoloft, Celexa, Paxil)**
- **Antacid drugs (H-2 blockers and PPI's such as Nexium, Prilosec, and Zantac)**
- **Osteoporosis drugs (Bisphosphonates such as Fosomax and Actonel, Zometa, and Boniva)**
- **Diabetes drugs (Metformin, Avandia, Glucotrol, etc.)**

- Anti-inflammatory drugs (Celebrex, Vioxx, Motrin, Naprosyn, etc)
- Synthetic Hormones (Provera and Estrogen)

SALT YOUR WAY TO HEALTH, 2nd Edition

Dr. Brownstein dispels many of the myths of salt. Salt is bad for you. Salt causes hypertension. These are just a few of the myths Dr. Brownstein tackles in this book. He shows you how the right kind of salt--unrefined salt--can have a remarkable health benefit to the body. Refined salt is a toxic, devitalized substance for the body. Unrefined salt is a necessary ingredient for achieving your optimal health. See how adding unrefined salt to your diet can help you:

- Maintain a normal blood pressure
- Balance your hormones
- Optimize your immune system
- Lower your risk for heart disease
- Overcome chronic illness

THE MIRACLE OF NATURAL HORMONES, 3RD EDITION

Optimal health cannot be achieved with an imbalanced hormonal system. Dr. Brownstein's research on bioidentical hormones provides the reader with a plethora of information on the benefits of balancing the hormonal system with bioidentical, natural hormones. This book is in its third edition. This book gives actual case studies of the benefits of natural hormones.

See how balancing the hormonal system can help:
- Arthritis and autoimmune disorders
- Chronic fatigue syndrome and fibromyalgia
- Heart disease
- Hypothyroidism
- Menopausal symptoms
- And much more!

OVERCOMING ARTHRITIS

Dr. Brownstein shows you how a holistic approach can help you overcome arthritis, fibromyalgia, chronic fatigue syndrome, and other conditions. This approach encompasses the use of:
- **Allergy elimination**
- Detoxification
- Diet
- Natural, bioidentical hormones
- Vitamins and minerals
- Water

THE GUIDE TO HEALTHY EATING, 2nd Edition

Which food do you buy? Where to shop? How do you prepare food? This book will answer all of these questions and much more. Dr. Brownstein co-authored this book with his nutritionist, Sheryl Shenefelt, C.N. Eating the healthiest way is the most important thing you can do. This book contains recipes and information on how best to feed your family.

See how eating a healthier diet can help you:

- Avoid chronic illness
- Enhance your immune system
- Improve your family's nutrition

THE GUIDE TO A GLUTEN-FREE DIET, 2nd Edition

What would you say if 16% of the population (1/6) had a serious, life-threatening illness that was only being diagnosed correctly only 3% of the time? Gluten-sensitivity is the most frequently missed diagnosis in the U.S. This book will show how you can incorporate a healthier lifestyle by becoming gluten-free.
- Why you should become gluten-free
- What illnesses are associated with gluten sensitivity
- How to shop and cook gluten-free
- Where to find gluten-free resources

THE GUIDE TO A DAIRY-FREE DIET

This book will show you why dairy is not a healthy food. Dr. Brownstein and Sheryl Shenefelt, C.N., will provide you the information you need to become dairy free. This book will dispel the myth that dairy from pasteurized milk is a healthy food choice. In fact, it is a devitalized food source which needs to be avoided.

Read this book to see why common dairy foods including milk cause:
- Osteoporosis
- Diabetes
- Allergies
- Asthma
- A Poor Immune System

Call 1-888-647-5616 or send a check or money order
BOOKS $15 each!

Sales Tax: For Michigan residents, please add $.90 per book.

Shipping:		
	1-3 Books	$5.00
	4-5 Books:	$4.00
	6-8 Books:	$3.00
	9 Books:	FREE SHIPPING!

VOLUME DISCOUNTS AVAILABLE.
CALL 1-888-647-5616 FOR MORE DETAILS

DVD's of Dr. Brownstein's Latest Lectures Available!
INFORMATION OR ORDER ON-LINE AT:
WWW.DRBROWNSTEIN.COM

You can also send a check to:
Medical Alternatives Press
4173 Fieldbrook
West Bloomfield, MI 48323

More about soy and this book at www.thesoydeception.com